"*Martin Sheen: Pilgrim on the Way* is a celebrity biography unlike any other, and for one simple reason: it has a soul. Sister Rose Pacatte captures more than Sheen's well-known career trajectory; she also infuses his story with something akin to grace. More than an actor's rise to fame, this is the story of a pilgrim's progress—a stirring and inspiring glimpse into one man's journey of faith that will resonate with seekers of all kinds."

—Deacon Greg Kandra
  Journalist and blogger, *The Deacon's Bench*

"Without sentimentality, Rose Pacatte's biography of Martin Sheen is insightful, intelligent, and funny—like the man whose story it narrates. The book opens with a story of Sheen's First Communion—and in a very tangible way, this eucharistic theme continues to unfold throughout the book. Not only because of Martin's love for the Mass and the Blessed Sacrament, but perhaps most telling, because of his keen understanding and certainty in God's presence in the living Body of Christ—in humanity. The man who confesses he's 'still astonished at the gift of the Eucharist' and admits that he 'counts on the sacraments for joy,' is also the award-winning Hollywood actor striving to live out his Catholic faith as a disciple of Jesus with deliberate intent, integrity and action. What an inspiring story!"

—María Ruiz Scaperlanda
  Author and blogger at *Day by Day with Maria*

"Knowing Martin Sheen through his acting and his Catholic activism, it was a treat to read Rose Pacatte's portrait and delve deeper into the life of this most remarkable man. Pacatte, who knows both the Hollywood and Catholic scenes, is the perfect person to write this book and she does so simply and cleanly. I came away from reading her portrait enriched and more hopeful about human possibilities, about virtue, and the way goodness can break through pain. A true spirit accomplishment."

—Tom Fox
  Publisher, *National Catholic Reporter*

Martin Sheen

Pilgrim on the Way

Rose Pacatte

LITURGICAL PRESS
Collegeville, Minnesota

www.litpress.org

Cover design by Stefan Killen Design. Cover illustration by Philip Bannister.

1   2   3   4   5   6   7   8   9

Library of Congress Control Number: 2014950490

ISBN 978-0-8146-3712-8   978-0-8146-3737-1 (ebook)

Contents

Acknowledgments

When I contacted Martin Sheen about writing this biography, he graciously agreed to a lengthy interview with the possibility of a follow-up. He then sent me a copy of Jim Hargrove's *Martin Sheen: Actor and Activist*, published in 1991 by Children's Press (an imprint now owned by Scholastic) for junior and high school students. Martin said that this was the most accurate and best researched account of his life to date. I have taken quotes from Hargrove's book and referred to it often. Thank you, Jim.

Along the Way: The Journey of a Father and a Son is another source I have consulted and quoted from for this biography. It is, by far, the most intimate and detailed account of Martin's life, from his perspective and that of his eldest son, Emilio.

But the most interesting—and entertaining—sources for this book are the interviews given me by Martin, his sister Carmen Estevez Phelan (whom I call the "memory keeper" of the family), and his brothers Frank, John, and Joe Estevez. I interviewed Martin at his home in Malibu, California, and his brothers Frank and John at the University of Dayton in a conference room that Sister Angela Ann Zukowski, MHSH, of the Center for Pastoral Initiatives graciously made available to us. Carmen, who lives in Spain, responded in depth by email to my initial list of questions and then confirmed facts or provided new information in many subsequent emails we exchanged throughout the writing project. Everyone should have a generous sister like Carmen. I interviewed Joe, who lives in Southern California, by phone.

I want to thank the following people who gave their time and input through writing, by phone, or in person: Rev. John Dear, author and activist; Elizabeth McAlister, of Jonah House; Douglas Kmiec, retired US Ambassador to Malta; Rev. William F. Kerze, Pastor of Our Lady of Malibu Parish, Malibu, California; Msgr. Lloyd Torgerson, Pastor of St. Monica's Parish, Santa Monica, California; Matt Clark, actor; Michael R. Rhodes, director and producer; Rev. Frank Desiderio, CSP, former president of Paulist Productions; Paul Chavez, president of the Cesar Chavez Foundation; Arturo Rodriguez, president of the United Farm Workers; Roy Bourgeois, founder of School of the Americas Watch; Helena Buscema, singer and songwriter; Rev. Ron Schmidt, SJ, documentary producer, Hope Media Productions; Rev. Michael Kennedy, SJ, executive director of Jesuit Restorative Justice Initiative; Jeff Dietrich, author and Catholic Worker, Los Angeles and his wife Catherine Morris, also a Catholic Worker; Blase Bonpane and Theresa Bonpane, founders of the Office of the Americas; Gerry Straub of Serving the Poor through the Power of Film; Carla Ward, cast member of *The West Wing* and my friend screenwriter Brian Oppenheimer who got the ball rolling.

I would like to give special thanks to my longtime friend Francine DeKom who gave me a quiet place in Maui to write for a month in the summer of 2014; my religious community, the Daughters of St. Paul in Culver City, California, who always support me; and my Catholics in Media colleagues of the greater Los Angeles area and beyond—you know who you are.

Abbreviations

CBS	Columbia Broadcasting System
CCNV	Community for Creative Non-Violence
NBC	National Broadcasting Company
NCR	National Cash Register Company
OFM	Order of Friars Minor (Franciscans)
OOA	Office of the Americas
OSU	Order of St. Ursula
MM	Maryknoll or Catholic Foreign Mission Society of America or Maryknoll Sisters of St. Dominic
PBS	Public Broadcasting Service
SJ	Society of Jesus (Jesuits)
SOA	School of the Americas

Introduction

Saints are celebrities for Catholics, and Martin Sheen is a Catholic who is a celebrity. The challenge to a Catholic author writing a biography about a living Catholic is twofold: to avoid making it sound like a eulogy and to escape hagiography, that is, writing as if the person were already a saint. I hope I have avoided these tendencies here—though my admiration for Martin Sheen's way of being Catholic is surely obvious.

That said, it is very difficult to find something negative to say about Martin Sheen as a person. This is, after all, a biograpy, not a tabloid scoop or a tell all. His past is well known. So here are all the ways Martin's friends and family members think he needs to improve today: Matt Clark, his friend since 1959, thinks Martin should spend more time at home with his wife and family. Ambassador in retirement, Douglas W. Kmiec, and others think he really, really needs to use a computer and email so they can stay in touch better. Martin's youngest brother, Joe, would like to be closer to his brother. Martin's son Emilio found it very difficult to direct his father in *The Way* (2010) because he was so easily distracted by people who recognized him—and he was willing to shake hands and speak with each one! Martin admits to being an intrepid storyteller (well, he says "blowhard"). Professionally, Martin admits that he acted in many films and television shows over the years, not because they were quality projects, but for the work, for a paycheck—he had a family to support. When I asked Martin about the ubiquitous commercial he narrated for Centrum Silver®, a multivitamin for adults 50+ now airing on television, he said, "But I only do commercials for products I believe in."

As a Catholic writer I have taken care to protect the privacy of Martin's family members, especially that of his children and grandchildren.

What makes Martin Sheen a solid candidate for a living biography is the arc of his life journey, his struggles and reversion to the practice of his faith in such meaningful ways. It is all part of his commitment to the pilgrim's journey, the way he strives to live an integrated personal and public, active, Catholic life.

I have included extended quotes from Martin's family and many of the activists who have marched with Martin, and his friends. Their warm and sometimes humorous memories tell stories that have not been yet heard.

Martin Sheen's thoughts on social justice have not been collected and widely published, though his poignant memoir with son Emilio, *Along the Way: The Journey of a Father and Son,* is available, and I recommend it.[1] Interviews with Martin Sheen abound in print and online. One of the best ways to grasp his thought on Catholic social activism is to examine the forewords he has authored for books written by his friends and social justice colleagues, such as those referred to in this book.

Martin Sheen is beloved in Los Angeles, a fact that was reinforced when I visited Dr. Barbara Giesser, my neurologist at the University of California. I have relapsing-remitting MS (multiple sclerosis), the same as the fictional President Josiah Bartlet, played by Martin Sheen on *The West Wing*. At my semiannual checkup, Dr. Giesser, who is the vice-chair of the Neurology Department at UCLA's Ronald Reagan Medical Center in Los Angeles, asked me what I had been doing lately. I told her I had just finished writing a biography of Martin Sheen. Imagine my surprise when she said very excitedly, "But I am his neurologist!" That is she consulted with him about his character, President Bartlet, who had MS on *The West Wing*. She spoke with him once by phone and twice consulted on the set at the Warner Bros. lot in Burbank. Dr. Giesser said, "He was very presidential when he was in character. He gave me a tour of the set and is one of the most considerate, courteous, and gracious individuals I have ever met. He went out of his busy way to make me feel comfortable and introduce me to his colleagues. I will never forget his kindness. I think there is an old saying about celebrities that goes something along the lines of 'the bigger they are, the nicer they are.' Mr. Sheen really epitomized that for me."

Martin's foreword to Jeff Dietrich's *Broken and Shared: Food, Dignity, and the Poor on Los Angeles' Skid Row* sums up Martin's core values well:

> Even for the most conservative among us there is little doubt that we are all responsible for each other, and the world is exactly the way it is because consciously, or unconsciously, we have made it so. But as things decline more and more rapidly with the world's economy in shambles, very few are aware of just how devastating the residual effects are on the poor who are ground down and served up daily to the gods of our idolatry: perpetual war, corporate greed, and personal indifference.
>
> Clearly the need to bring compassion, peace-making, and social justice into the fray has never been greater, but

when faced with such a reality, who can be blamed for turning away in despair or self-preservation? And yet the open invitation from the gospel still reached our heart after 2,000 years and we are left to wonder: Whatever you did to the least of mine you have done to me.

Simply stated, this is the story of Jeff Dietrich's lifelong effort to unite the will of the spirit with the work of the flesh . . .[2]

It is also Martin Sheen's lifelong quest, this search for God, for transcendence, and to unite the will of the spirit to the work of the flesh. His is an ongoing program of life that he strives to live and witness joyfully to faith, hope, and love in the world.

Why does Martin Sheen do what he does? "I do it because I can't seem to live with myself if I do not. I don't know any other way to be. It isn't something you can explain; it is just something that you do; it is something that you are."[3]

The best book about Martin Sheen is yet to be written, but with a community of Martin's family and friends, I have tried to make *Martin Sheen: Pilgrim on the Way* the best it can be.

CHAPTER ONE

The Pilgrimage Begins

If you ask actor Martin Sheen if he remembers his First Communion in the spring of 1948 he will answer with a resounding, "I sure do!" followed by laughter, tinged with mischief and maybe a little sadness.

He and his mother, Mary Ann, set out for Holy Trinity Parish in Dayton, Ohio, under a cloudy sky. He was dressed in white, and his mother was sporting a new hat for the occasion. After Mass he and his mother headed toward the church hall for the traditional breakfast when it began to sprinkle. She handed Martin her umbrella, and he ran off to be with his friends leaving his mother to fend for herself.

When Martin arrived home quite a while after Mary Ann did—and with no umbrella—his mother said, "Where did you go? I looked everywhere for you! You took the umbrella and now my new hat is ruined!"

Martin Sheen was born Ramon Gerard Estevez on August 3, 1940, in Dayton, Ohio. Martin Sheen is the name he took for himself when he began acting in New York in 1959. Antonio is his confirmation name, and his brother Mike was his sponsor. What he remembers most about his confirmation is the preparation: "It was kind of militaristic, with all these heroic images of how our lives were to be and how we were to be like St. George slaying dragons to further the faith. I must have been twelve or thirteen when I was confirmed."

In a 2003 *Inside the Actors Studio* interview, Martin talked in depth about changing his name to Martin Sheen, which is a combination of the names of the CBS casting director who gave him his first break (Robert Dale Martin) and a certain Catholic televangelist whom he considered "a magnificent actor" (Archbishop Fulton J. Sheen).

> Whenever I would call for an appointment, whether it was a job or an apartment, and I would give my name, there was always that hesitation and when I'd get there, it was always gone. So I thought, I got enough problems trying to get an acting job, so I invented Martin Sheen. It's still Estevez officially. I never changed it officially. I never will. It's on my driver's license and passport and everything. I started using Sheen, I thought I'd give it a try, and before I knew it, I started making a living with it and then it was too late. In fact, one of my great regrets is that I didn't keep my name as it was given to me. I knew it bothered my dad."[1]

Martin Sheen's father was Francisco Estevez who was born on June 2, 1898, in the village of Parderrubias in the province of Galicia, Spain. He was the eldest of seven children and grew up very poor. Francisco's father and Martin's grandfather, Manuel Estevez, grew grapes for wine and other produce, and raised chickens for the family and to sell. His grandmother, Dolores Martinez, augmented the family income using her sewing machine. Francisco became the head of the family when his father died. The youngest brother, Matías, was an active anti-Fascist but was falsely accused of certain anti-Franco activities at the beginning of the Spanish Civil War (1936–1939) and spent several years in prison and designated a Communist. For years after his release he remained on a kind of probation as long as Franco was in power. Because of his political record he was never allowed to leave Spain.

Several of Francisco's brothers and relatives emigrated to the United States, South America, and Cuba in the early 1900s to work and raise their families. Francisco left Spain for Cuba with two of his cousins from the same village. After working for several years in the sugar cane fields he became a Cuban national. With his savings he went to the United States. Records show that he entered the country in 1919 through Philadelphia (or Miami, accounts differ) and made his way to Dayton, Ohio, where, he was told, many factory jobs were available. After working for a while as a janitor at the National Cash Register Company (NCR) he saved some money and went to Mexico City, planning to start a business as a street vendor. However, the bank in Dayton that was to transfer his savings to a Mexican bank failed to do so. Soon, Francisco was back in Dayton and was able to recover his savings. He again worked for NCR, a major employer in town, famous for making the first mechanical cash registers in 1884. He would spend the rest of his life working for NCR as a highly skilled machinist and quality control supervisor in Dayton and in other countries.

Mary Ann Phelan, Martin's mother, was born in Borrisokane, County Tipperary, Ireland, on May 22, 1903. Her family owned a pub in the village. She completed school at age sixteen. Her brother Michael was active in the Irish Republican Army, and Mary Ann carried messages for the IRA in the tubes of her bicycle during the years leading up to the Irish War of Independence (1919–21). Michael also seems to have been an actor, though it is not clear to what extent.

After leaving school, Mary Ann went England to take a secretarial course and then headed to the United States, entering via Ellis Island on May 10, 1921, to live with relatives in Dayton, Ohio.

Both of Martin Sheen's parents left their countries of origin for opportunity; for Mary Ann especially, her family's political leanings made immigration a very good idea.

Mary Ann lived with relatives in Dayton's east end and earned her way, in part, by keeping house for them but they treated her like a servant. She soon found a job and took a room at a respectable boarding house, to the great disapproval of her uncle. Good Catholic girls did not do that. But Mary Ann knew who she was and was very independent. Francisco and Mary Ann met when taking citizenship classes. Francisco had little formal education, spoke little English, and was slight of stature, perhaps about five feet six. Mary Ann was a pretty, pleasingly plump Irish lass, about five feet two, who spoke English and Gaelic. They fell in love and married at St. Joseph's Church on Monday, September 5, 1927.

Francisco Estevez never missed a day of work in his life, according to his children. On the day he and Mary Ann were married at a 6:00 a.m. Mass, family lore says he was at work by 7:00 a.m.

Full House

Their first child, Dolores, named for Francisco's mother, was born on January 20, 1929, and only lived a day or two. A poignant family story tells of Francisco holding a tiny coffin on his lap in a taxi as he and Mary Ann made their way to arrange for her burial. Dolores is buried in Calvary Cemetery in Dayton.

Francisco and Mary Ann then moved to Colombia for NCR, living in both Bucaramanga and Bogota. After losing another son who was stillborn, they became pregnant again, and Mary Ann decided to return to Ireland for the birth of her child. She did not speak Spanish, and according to her daughter Carmen, Mary Ann wanted to give birth where she was more comfortable. In addition, she was worried about her own mother's health. She told Francisco that they would reunite when he found work in a more civilized place.

Mary Ann gave birth to Manuel Noel on December 14, 1929, in Borrisokane, County Tipperary, Ireland (d. August 28, 1968, Pasadena, CA).

Two years later NCR sent Francisco to Hamilton, Bermuda, and Mary Ann joined him there. Miguel "Mike" Jude was born on August 4, 1933 (d. July 12, 1981, Los Angeles, CA). He was followed by Conrad Joseph on March 26, 1935 (d. November 1998, Dayton, OH); Carlos Patrick on April 25, 1936 (d. May 25, 2010, Brownsville, TX); Francisco "Frank" Vincent on July 21, 1937; and Alfonso "Al" Navarre on May 8, 1939 (d. August 27, 2002, Dayton, OH).

By this time the Nazi threat was looming, and on September 3, 1939, Britain and France declared war on Germany following Germany's invasion of Poland. Also on that day the Germans sunk the British ship SS *Athenia* off the coast of Ireland. Germany only had fifty submarines at that time but had begun attacking British shipping. It was time for the Estevez family to return to Dayton.

Ramon Gerard, the future Martin Sheen, was born there on August 3, 1940. His left arm was crushed by the use of forceps during birth, leaving his arm about two inches shorter than the other, a challenge he deftly overcame so that even today it is hardly noticeable. It also did not prevent him from becoming a caddie at the age of nine and working to help out his family and support himself once he left home to become an actor.

The family settled in at 751 Brown Street in the South Park neighborhood near downtown Dayton and not far from church, schools, the University of Dayton, and NCR. The Dayton Country Club golf course, on the line between Kettering and Oakwood, where all the boys would caddy, was either a really long walk when the boys didn't have bus fare or short bus ride from their home when they did. The Brown Street house was the Estevez family home until the city claimed it by eminent domain. A few days after the last born son, Joe, graduated from high school in 1964 and left home, the city demolished the house. Today it is an empty lot.

Nevertheless in 1940 it was indeed a full house and becoming fuller by the year.

Carmen was born on February 9, 1942, the first girl after seven sons in a row. Francisco, or "Pop" as the Estevez children still refer to their dad (and how I will refer to him throughout this book), got to work two hours late that day, surprising the large group of men he worked with at NCR, because Pop was never late. In fact, he got up early every morning to get to work and prepare for the day. The men had known Mary Ann and Francisco were expecting, and when they heard the couple now had a daughter they burst into a loud round of applause.

John Barry was born on May 9, 1943, followed by Joseph "Joe" Walter on February 13, 1946. John eventually became a DJ and radio broadcaster and went on to work in public television. Joe is the only one to become an actor like Martin.

Carmen Estevez Phelan, the surviving girl in the family, is a teacher in Spain and the "memory keeper" for much of the family history. Pop told Carmen that her mother was the one who chose the names for the children. While it may seem

Mary Ann chose a Spanish first name and an English middle name for many of the children to acknowledge their families of origin, her reasons were quite varied—though she liked Spanish names. Carmen recalls what Pop once explained to her about how the Estevez children got their names. It offers an affectionate look into a marriage:

> Manuel was named after Pop's father, Manuel, according to the Spanish tradition. However, our mother wanted to call him Noel as that is Irish for Manuel: "God is with us." They could not come to an agreement, so Manuel became Manuel Noel. She gave the second son the name Michael, like her father and brother, but in Spanish it is Miguel. Mike's second name is Jude because he almost died at birth, and my mother had a great devotion to St. Jude, the patron saint of hopeless cases. Conrad was Conrad Joseph because my mother's favorite author when he was born was Joseph Conrad. Carlos is Carlos because she liked that name and his middle name is Patrick. Of course, she had to give that very Irish name to at least one of her children. Francisco is Francisco because this time Pop insisted that it was time for him to have a namesake. Frank's middle name is Vincent, not for anyone but because our mother liked that name. Alfonso is another name she liked, and Al's middle name is Navarre because our mother's favorite actor at that time was Ramon Navarro. Ramon, a.k.a. Martin, is Ramon because of my mother's favorite actor. Did this name have anything to do with him becoming an actor? Who knows? His was a difficult birth and a certain Sister Gerard was very helpful. My mother was grateful and she gave Ramon "Gerard" as a middle name to honor that nun. My name is Carmen because I am named after Pop's only sister, and I have no middle name because she did not have one either. John is John Barry after a famous naval hero. Joe is Joseph because I think both of our parents had a special devotion

to St. Joseph, and they were married in Dayton at St. Joseph's Church. His middle name, Walter, is after his godfather, but Joe says the name is not on his birth certificate. So Pop had some choices but most of the names are from an Irish lady who liked romantic, nice-sounding names.

School Days

The Estevez boys were a rowdy, disruptive lot and became more so as they grew older. Yet they were raised in a disciplined, thoroughly Catholic family, and all received an excellent Catholic education for twelve years. The boys were altar servers. And all the children of Francisco and Mary Ann would have trouble with alcohol.

In Bermuda the boys attended Mt. St. Agnes Academy, run by the Sisters of Charity of St. Vincent De Paul of Halifax, Nova Scotia. Later on, after retiring as a teacher and counselor, Frank would return to Mt. St. Agnes to teach. In Dayton the children attended Holy Trinity for grade school and the boys Chaminade High School, run by the Society of Mary or Marianists. Carmen graduated from Julienne High School, run by the Sisters of Notre Dame de Namur.[2] Some of the Estevez children attended the University of Dayton as undergrads or for postgraduate courses or degrees. Today, at least two of Martin Sheen's nieces or great-nieces work at the university.

Frank is the only one to graduate from a public high school, however. After an altercation with a Chaminade basketball coach halfway through his senior year, he was expelled and finished up at the local public high school. Frank does not have fond memories of Chaminade nor the school's teaching methods as they applied to him.

Martin received his diploma in 1958 with his class, but it was blank. He had failed science and Pop "was furious."[3]

Getting an education and going to work in the factory was of paramount importance to Pop. A priest mentor and friend, Fr. Alfred Drapp, the associate pastor at Holy Trinity, convinced Martin to go to summer school and get his diploma. Drapp also encouraged Martin to take the entrance exams for the University of Dayton in order to please his father. Martin was close to Fr. Al and had served his Masses since Father first came to the parish when Martin was fourteen. So Martin listened, got his high school diploma, took the exam for the University of Dayton, and deliberately failed it. He wanted to be an actor and figured you didn't need an education to do it. He had a change of heart decades later, and in 2006 he studied for a term at the National University in Galway, Ireland, and seemed to enjoy it very much.[4]

Growing up in the Estevez household was a challenge. There was not a lot of space and there was little money. They had a radio but they did not have a television until much later. Frank recalls his mother sending him to the store and always reminding him "not to tarry" on the way home—and to bring her all the change, even if it was just a few pennies. Pop was a very strict disciplinarian and frequently reminded his kids that they were knuckleheads and hooligans, which by their own admission, they were. Both Frank and John attest to the two-family idea, which when children are born before a significant event or gap in years, sibling memories differ. For the Estevez children, Bermuda was the dividing line. The eldest from that time still living, Frank, remembers his family history, and even some shared events, differently than Martin, Carmen, John, and Joe who were born after the family returned to Dayton.

Frank emphasizes how poor the family was, and of this the siblings agree. At Christmas, Pop would bring home a scrappy tree that only cost seventy-five cents or was abandoned on the lot. Frank thinks there was even a year when they had no tree. Carmen has fond memories, noting that even if there wasn't much money there was always a tree with a nativity set under it, and the family had fun decorating the tree. While their mother was alive she would buy small gifts or give money to the older boys to buy them. Then she would hide them around the house and, after the younger children would find and open them, she would rewrap them, hoping no one would notice. After Mary Ann's death, Pop would give the children money to buy Christmas gifts for everyone, mostly "socks, underwear, gloves, ties, pajamas, notebooks, school supplies, books, small toys, plastic cowboys and Indians, and board games." They would play the board games until all the pieces were lost. Carmen recalls her mother teaching them Christmas carols, especially her favorite, "Christmas Is Coming." When the kids still at home were teenagers they would go to Christmas midnight Mass. Carmen sang in the choir and remembers that the ushers would send people who were under the influence of alcohol to the choir loft during the Mass. Her brothers were often among them.

Martin remembers that the family was always on the verge of poverty and that one of the disadvantages to poverty is that "you develop a chip on your shoulder" and this means, "you don't give anyone else a break, especially wealthy people." Martin was a caddy from about the age of nine. "I really had it in for those rich people" at the country club. They pretended a caddy didn't exist and did not guard their speech. They were very stingy with tips so Martin started a caddy union and held a strike when he was turning fifteen in 1955. He admits he didn't know what he was doing but most of all he wanted to have "a voice" to unite the lads. The men and women they caddied for were wealthy, impossible to talk to, and used foul language, yet Martin saw something very vulnerable about them. Still he calls them "loafers" who were vulgar and who drank a lot. The men, mostly all professionals, played on Saturdays and Wednesdays and on many days in between, but on Sundays, when they played with their wives, "butter would melt in their mouths." To this day Martin does not play golf in private clubs unless it is for a charity tournament, as he has done for his parish in the Our Lady of Malibu Golf Classic, in Malibu, California. He doesn't play on public courses because people recognize him and it becomes difficult to play. As for the strike, the caddie master convinced most of the lads to come back to work and catch a round of golf before the end of the day. Martin and his brothers Al and Joe were fired but they eventually returned to work. It was Martin's first foray into social activism.

Martin's father called him "Rrrramon!" and his brothers and sister still call him "Roman" probably based on the way their Irish mother pronounced his name, a cross between Raymond and Ramon. "Ray" was another nickname for him. He wore glasses and some of the kids, including his brothers, called him "Four Eyes" that turned into "Eyes." Another moniker that his father, brothers, and fellow caddies used for Martin was "Isaac," though his brother Joe and sister Carmen don't agree on the origin of that nickname.

With such a large family, the money Martin and his brothers earned as caddies, especially over the hot and humid summer months, helped to pay their tuitions and to buy uniforms.

When a Mother Dies

Mary Ann Phelan Estevez died suddenly on August 1, 1951, of a cerebral hemorrhage. She was sitting in her rocking chair in the bedroom and praying the rosary when the end came. She had grown stout in previous years and was not able to get around very well in the last two. She was only forty-eight years old. At the time of her death, Conrad was seventeen, Carlos was sixteen, Frank was fifteen, Al was thirteen, Martin was eleven, Carmen was nine, John was eight, and Joe was just five years old. Of all the surviving Estevez siblings, Joe remembers his mother the least.

Manuel, the eldest surviving child, had been drafted into the army but was classified 4F because he did not meet the physical standards for recruitment due to a heart murmur. After living in Mexico for some time to find work, he finally came home when Pop convinced Mary Ann to stop sending him money (Pop then sent him just enough to get to the US-Mexican border and then made his way home). Manuel was his mother's favorite, Carmen says, probably because he was her first child to survive. Manuel died of a massive coronary in 1968, leaving behind a wife and child born after his death. Mike had joined the Marines and was on his way to Korea when he got news of his mother's death.

According to all accounts, Mary Ann was a bit of a character. She was strong and loving and a great conversationalist with an excellent sense of humor. And like all the Estevez clan, she loved to tell stories and was known to break into a song if the moment was right. She taught her children to be fair and generous.

"But she was a very strict mother," says Carmen. "You never got away with anything and no matter how you tried to hide anything you had done, she always found out. On the other hand, she was the first to defend us all from anybody she thought was unfair or might hurt us. I have a very clear vision of her once in the back yard waving a carving knife in her hand warning somebody to never lay a hand on any of her children again. She was the one to punish her children and no one else!"

To make some extra money she worked at a pub every now and then, leaving the children in the care of her best friend, Mrs. Magnus, across the street. After Mary Ann's death Mrs. Magnus did what she could to help the family until she moved away.

Mary Ann was a woman of deep faith and led the family rosary every night, gathering the children around the dining room table. Sometimes during Lent they said three rosaries. As the boys got older they found reasons to be elsewhere when the rosary beads came out. For her entire life Mary Ann remained proud of her Irish roots.

One of Carmen's fondest memories is of her mother "sitting in her rocker and me unbraiding her thick, long black and silver hair. I can still feel my fingers running through the waves the braids had left. Then I would brush it and brush it and brush it until she would say, 'Okay, Carmen, that's grand. That's enough now.' And she never missed an episode of the radio show *Our Girl Sunday*."

Mary Ann's death left Pop to care for eight children still at home, and he never waivered. Pop was a responsible man, and he expected his children to become responsible adults, though this was a long time coming for some of them. People were surprised that he didn't send the children to an orphanage. Though, as the only girl he considered sending Carmen away to boarding school, believing that the nuns would know how to raise such a willful child. When she accused Pop of wanting to send her away because he did not love her, he gave in and kept her at home. Carmen couldn't imagine being away from him and her brothers.

Pop was up early every morning to what Frank and John refer to as "Pop time," that is, always earlier than anyone else thought necessary. He would check the bulletin each week for the altar server schedule and then would wake up those who were scheduled to serve Mass and make sure they had breakfast. Then he would leave for work. The children took turns cooking dinner, and he gave them the money to buy the necessary groceries. He also made sure they got to doctor and dentist appointments. Frank recalls someone asking why Pop never remarried and his response: "Who would marry a man with ten kids?"

After Mary Ann died, an air of sadness and gloom dominated the house. Pop was probably depressed but they didn't have the word for it back then. There was a lot of anger, and the kids fought as usual, but the fights seemed to last longer now that their mother was not there to mediate. School, homework, work, and chores continued, which created a sense of normalcy. They tried to keep in mind that their mother was looking down on them from heaven and this helped the children behave to a certain extent. "It took us all a long time to get used to being without a mother, and I think maybe we never really did. She was always with us even though she left us when she was very young," according to Carmen.

In his son Emilio Estevez's fictional 2010 film *The Way*, Martin Sheen plays a widower, Tom, who is making the pilgrimage to Santiago de Compostela, carrying the ashes of his estranged son. Tom tells a story to a fellow pilgrim, Sarah (Deborah Kara Unger), about a lesson learned from his mother when he once hit his sister: only cowards hit women. It's a true story. Martin had been chasing Carmen alongside the house one day intending to catch her and hit her when suddenly a window flew open and a mop landed on Martin's head. He and Carmen looked up and saw their mother looking down at them and listened as she said the now famous words: "Only cowards hit women." Martin never hit Carmen again. In fact, Al and Martin defended the younger kids when the older boys picked on them.

Carmen remembers Martin as being his own person and also the heated arguments the kids would get into at the breakfast table after Pop left for work. One day Conrad was nagging Martin about his long hair and the way he dressed when the two brothers started circling the table. After giving Conrad a piece of his mind, Martin ran out the back door, "sailed over the porch railing, landed in Mrs. Monahan's back yard, and kept running."

As the years passed for the Estevez family after their mother died, the kids went to school; Pop continued work at NCR, pacing the floor and stirring his coffee when at home, two distinct habits the siblings recall about him. On Sunday afternoons the kids always went to the movies at the nearby Sigma Theater. After the movies they would act them out in the back yard or in the front room, using the sliding inner doors as a curtain. And they finally got a television set.

At one point Manuel was jailed after hitting several parked cars while driving drunk, and it was Martin who got the bail money together. Mike joined the marine corps, Carlos and Alfonso joined the navy, Conrad lived at home and worked at NCR, and Martin realized he wanted to be an actor more than anything else. It would not be easy.

CHAPTER TWO

An Actor on the Way

Martin knew he wanted to become an actor from at least the age of seven when he first started going to the movies.[1] One of Martin's first acting gigs was in 1953 for Ohio's 150th celebration of statehood. He was in eighth grade and played a priest for the first time (he would go on to play a priest in several films and television programs). Carmen played a mother, and they shared one scene together.

In high school he would stand on a crate to recite poetry and by the time he was a junior he had acted in about a dozen school plays. While making up classes during the summer of 1958 so he could finally get his high school diploma, Martin auditioned for a local television talent show called *The Rising Generation*.[2]

Contestants for the show were the usual suspects who sang, danced, and performed magic tricks and comedy routines, but Martin wanted to showcase his acting ability. He read a poem by James Weldon Johnson (1871–1938), the first African-American professor at New York University, called *The Creation*, based on the biblical book of Genesis. Today, audiences vote for talent or reality show winners via mobile phone, texting, and social media, but in those days people wrote the name of their choice on a postcard and sent it into the station. Martin won that week and then he won the finals. The grand prize was a five-day trip to New York for two and a chance to audition at the CBS television network headquarters in Manhattan.

Accompanied by his older brother Manuel, Martin experienced his first flight on an airplane in September. Once in New York he auditioned for a CBS casting director by the name of Robert Dale Martin, who was very supportive. He liked Martin's baritone voice and suggested that his prospects for an acting career would be better served in New York than Dayton. When Martin returned to New York within a few months to pursue acting, he discovered that a Hispanic name did not seem to open doors for him. So he took the stage name Martin Sheen, "Martin" for the kindly Robert D. Martin who had advised him at CBS and "Sheen" for the famous Catholic televangelist, Bishop Fulton J. Sheen (1895–1979).[3]

New York

Pop was very worried about Martin leaving home to become an actor. He was even willing to pay Martin's tuition to the University of Dayton because of his shortened left arm, thinking it a handicap, but Martin would have nothing of it. Once Martin left for New York by bus on January 31, 1959, Pop would tell the kids still at home that he hoped Martin would get the nonsense out of his system and come home and get a normal job. It never happened.

Martin sold his class ring, and Fr. Drapp, from Holy Trinity Parish, loaned Martin three hundred dollars, enough money to get him started in New York. The priest would send him more periodically. Martin's first home was a tiny room in a boarding house near St. Stephen's Catholic Church at 131 East 30th Street in Manhattan. Then, like most aspiring actors even today, Martin began working a series of night jobs, such as a stock boy at American Express, so he could go to auditions during the day. In the beginning he went to Mass occasionally and then just stopped going.

Despite working hard, Martin never had much money and was often hungry. His brother Frank recalls visiting him there when he was in the army. "Pop wrote to me that Martin had gone and done it—that is, gone to New York to become an actor. I told Pop I would try my best to find him on one of my rotations back to the United States from where I was stationed in Germany." Frank took the bus from Fort Dix to the Port Authority bus station in midtown Manhattan. He found Martin living in a small room with a single bed and a dresser with three or four drawers and sharing a bathroom with the other boarders. "You don't have to live like this! Why don't you go home?" Frank asked Martin, implying "Who do you think you are anyway?" But Martin was firm, "I'm staying here until I make it." Frank admits he didn't know what Martin meant by "making it," if it meant Broadway or television, but "I had to admire him. I had some money and I tried to give it to him, but he wouldn't take it—even though he had these pitiful little jobs, working nights unloading trains and eating at the Salvation Army."

As an aspiring actor, Martin should have been taking acting lessons to better his chances but without money it was impossible. Along with other young actors, he cofounded the Actor's Co-op in a rented space near the old Madison Square Garden at 49th and 50th streets in Manhattan. Barbra Streisand was one of those young actors as was John Evans. Evans was leaving a backstage job at The

Living Theatre in Greenwich Village and suggested that Martin might like to take his place. The Living Theatre was an expressionist and unconventional troupe started by Julian Beck and Judith Malina in 1947. Martin and the future Oscar-winner Al Pacino worked as prop masters and stage-hands, and Martin was soon the janitor for the entire building, working for a very low wage. Martin also worked with Henry Proach at the Living Theatre and they became friends until Henry's death in 1986.

Martin's first break came when he was asked to play a role in one of a series of one-act plays held on Monday nights, when the theater was dark. It was the first time he was paid for acting, but the meager five dollars for each performance brought him face-to-face with real poverty because he had to give up his night job. The productions performed at The Living Theatre often carried ethical, social, and political messages that influenced Martin. He said in 2003 that working at The Living Theatre "had a very profound effect on me. I started with them when I was nineteen and spent two-and-a-half years with them. Through them, I was introduced to Women's Strike for Peace, the Ban the Bomb movement. It was an avant-garde theater, filled with very liberal, progressive, intelligent, passionate, heroic people. Julian Beck was one of my mentors and heroes. He introduced me to the Catholic Worker Movement."[4] Julian had told him about the free meals there. Martin finally landed a role in *The Connection,* a play about the dire effects of drug addiction. Martin played Ernie, a drug addict. It was one of the most successful and long running plays staged by The Living Theatre, and Martin made thirty dollars for each performance.

Martin has remained friends with Matt Clark, another aspiring actor he met at The Living Theatre in 1959. Matt remembers Martin eating free meals at the Catholic Worker

House on Chrystie Street in the Bowery where Martin volunteered to wash dishes and sell copies of the Catholic Worker newspaper for a penny apiece. Martin says that he may have met Dorothy Day: "But I never knew it. I went there for many months for food."

By the end of 1960, said Matt Clark, Martin was pulling the papers around in a wagon and dropping them off at newsstands.

"He had very little money," Matt recalls, "and often beggars who had more money than he did would stop and ask for change, and if Martin had it, he would give it. It drove me nuts. One time Martin gave a guy ten cents, and I decided to play a joke. As the man walked away I yelled out, 'You should ask him for more! He's got more!' and Martin gave the man everything he had. I thought I was teaching Martin a lesson but he wasn't impressed and I felt a proper fool. He was eighteen-years-old, and he was giving money away, everything he had."

Love, Marriage, Kids, and Career

Through a mutual friend at The Living Theatre, Martin met Janet Templeton, a young, aspiring artist and student at the New School for Social Research in Manhattan. Martin was smitten and he pursued her, though at first she was not impressed. About this time in 1961, Martin made his television debut in a series of small roles, beginning with *Route 66*. Some roles were recurring—an actor's dream. One of these was *The Defenders*, a drama series starring E.G. Marshall, Robert Reed, and Ossie Davis. Martin was in four episodes.

Martin's future wife was born in 1939 in Cincinnati, Ohio, to a single mother, Lena, who was from Salyersville, Kentucky. The town was in a very rural and mountainous region of the state, its population mostly Protestant fundamentalist. This is where her grandmother and two great-aunts, who were extremely religious, raised Janet for six years, while her mother went to Cleveland to work. When Lena came back to get her daughter, a custody battle ensued that her mother eventually won. She and Janet went to Cleveland, and some of the family followed. Although Lena was not as strict as the other relatives, she raised Janet as a Southern Baptist "and that meant no dancing, no makeup, no singing, and no fun," according to Martin. Until the age of eighteen, Janet would preach on street corners with her zealous half-sister, trying to save souls. Janet decided to become a nurse after high school and started taking classes on a scholarship at Western Reserve University (now Case Western Reserve) in Cleveland. When she realized this path was not making her happy, she earned a scholarship from the New School for Social Research to study art and moved to New York City. By this time Janet had had enough of organized religion.

Martin eventually won over Janet and moved in with her in the fall of 1960. But that didn't last long. The building superintendent soon evicted them for living in sin. Even with his Catholic and her Baptist upbringing, they were young and didn't really grasp why the building super had an issue with them living together. "What did us two kids really understand?" he said in an interview. The pair traveled together to Europe with The Living Theatre in the summer of 1961 when the company was asked to represent the United States in the Festival du Theatre des Nations in Paris. During the ten-city tour the couple got tickets to a general audience with Pope John XXIII in Rome, something Martin has never forgotten.

Already pregnant, the couple married on December 23, 1961, at St. Stephen's Catholic Church in Manhattan. In those days nuptial Masses were not permitted during Advent, so they were married in a quiet ceremony after the 8:00 a.m. Mass by the pastor, Father Patrick Fay. Although Janet agreed to be married in the Catholic church she had no desire to raise the children Catholic. Their first child and son, Emilio, was born about five months later on May 12, 1962. Martin didn't take the required childbirth classes so he was not allowed to be with Janet during the delivery, something he vowed never to let happen again—with interesting results when the second child came along the next year.

A Greek Catholic priest baptized the baby "Emilio Dominic" a few months later, at Martin's request. Emilio's middle name was to have been "Diogenes" but Martin got flustered when the priest asked for the middle name. Janet called Martin on his hypocrisy: living in sin one year and baptizing the baby the next. He was barely practicing his faith any more. Janet didn't really mind the baptism but she was afraid of Catholicism, thinking that as with her own religious upbringing, it would not allow a person to grow. Martin would have all his children baptized, though he says it was mostly for cultural reasons. Yet this was one part of his Catholic faith he did not skip over. "It was up to me to raise the children Catholic," Martin said, "and I did not follow through. Over the years, however, I would stop in at a Catholic church and notice the priest facing the people and eventually hear the priest say the words of Mass in English. I had been an altar boy and everything had been in Latin. This was new to me! So I didn't incorporate Vatican II in my life until I returned to the practice of the faith twenty years later."

The family was living in the Bronx when Emilio was born, and life with a baby was expensive, even with the help of donated baby clothes from the actors union. The small family was soon evicted for not paying rent, and they moved back to Dayton, hitching a ride with friends. Janet and Emilio stayed with Pop in the house on Brown Street for a few months while Martin returned to New York ahead of them. He rented a small apartment in an art deco building built in 1932, "The Ambassador" at 30 Daniel Low Terrace on Staten Island. It was a ten-minute walk to the ferry terminal and then a twenty-minute boat ride to Manhattan. This was the same apartment building where the actor Paul Newman and his first wife and child had lived in 1952. Martin also worked at a car wash on Bay Street for about six months.

In 1962–63 Martin appeared in various episodes of *Naked City*, *The United States Steel Hour*, *Armstrong Circle Theater*, and one episode of the cult classic, *The Outer Limits*. Martin made a guest appearance in the series *East Side/West Side* about New York's urban social problems. It was highly acclaimed, starred George C. Scott, and received a Primetime Emmy Award but only lasted one season.

Martin's career was beginning to take off.[5]

On August 3, 1963, their second child was born, Ramon Luis. It was quite an event. Since Martin had resolved never to miss another child's delivery, and because funds were low, they planned for a home birth but did not count on the midwife not being able to show up when they needed her. Martin delivered Ramon in their apartment but was not prepared for the rest of it. Woefully ignorant of the birthing process, once Ramon made his appearance Martin became afraid that Janet would hemorrhage and called an ambulance. All ended well.

Martin made his Broadway debut later that year at the Eugene O'Neill Theater in a mostly forgotten play, *Never Live Over a Pretzel Factory*. It opened and closed after nine performances. His next role, however, would earn him a Tony Award nomination in Frank D. Gilroy's Pulitzer Prize-winning play *The Subject Was Roses* that opened at the Royale Theater in May 1964. He played a young soldier returning home to navigate his parents' troubled marriage. Martin lost out to Jack Albertson who played his father in the play. When both actors reprised their roles for the film version in 1968, Albertson went on to win an Oscar and Martin a Golden Globe nomination. For many years following that first Tony Award nomination, Martin asked that his name be removed from nomination lists because "Competition in the arts is really at odds with what you're trying to do. It takes a group of people, a community of people, to present anything in the preforming arts. You can't do it on your own. Picking a specific person divides them from the effort it takes to be successful."[6]

Pop Comes to Visit

That same month his brother Joe graduated from high school, the house on Brown Street was no more, and Pop retired from NCR. One evening Pop called Martin to say he was coming to New York on his way to Spain, the first time he would visit home since he had left decades before. Martin got tickets for Pop and his brother Mike, who was living in Connecticut at the time, for a Tuesday performance of *The Subject Was Roses*. On Monday Martin learned that Lady Bird Johnson, the First Lady, with her daughters Lynda and Lucy, would be in attendance that night as well.

It would be the first time Pop would see Martin on stage. But when Martin told Pop that the First Lady would be there, he refused to go. His shy nature and stubbornness could not be overcome, so Martin had to exchange the tickets for the next evening instead. Martin recounts in *Along the Way*[7] his long wait for his father and brother to greet him in his dressing room after the play and how desperately he longed to hear words of encouragement from Pop. But neither the backstage visit nor those words from Pop, who had never given compliments to his children growing up, ever came. Pop and Mike returned to Martin and Janet's apartment without him. A week later, Pop left for Spain, and the silence lay heavy between father and son. However, Martin did give Pop a poster about the play as a memento. Martin and his siblings did not know when they would see Pop again as he intended to retire in Parderrubias where he had grown up. But it was not easy for Pop to be away from his family and the life to which he had become accustomed, and he returned to Dayton about six months later.

"It took Pop a really long time to get used to the fact that Martin was earning his bread as an actor," Carmen explains. "Pop was proud of him. We knew that. Once my brother Alfonso came home with a magazine and Pop asked him, 'Is your brother in that?' When Al answered in the negative, Pop asked, 'Well, why did you buy it then?' Pop did not brag much about his children."

The steady work from the play helped the financially struggling and growing family but it was never easy in those New York years. Carlos Irwin, known as Charlie Sheen today, was born on September 3, 1965, on Staten Island, and on April 2, 1967, their youngest child, a girl, Renée Pilar, was born in Manhattan. All the children would grow up to be actors.

Carmen went to visit Martin and his family in New York over Easter weekend in 1964, and Janet invited her to consider coming to live with them to care for the children. Carmen remembers:

Both Emilio and Ramon were young, and it was getting hard for Martin and Janet to go anywhere with two small children at home. Martin was in a Broadway show, his career was moving along, and there were social commitments that needed attention. At that time I had money saved, and I was planning to return to the University of Dayton full time. I had two years finished and had been working full time and doing some part time classes for two years, and I knew that if I did not go back now I would never get a degree. Janet was very convincing and she suggested going to school in New York. Janet sent me admission forms from various universities and one of them was New York University. They accepted me and gave me credit for a lot of the courses I had done at the University of Dayton. I continued as a part-time student but I was also a full-time nanny.

I can't tell you how living with my brother and his family changed my life. I took my new role very seriously, and I became very attached to Emilio and Ramon. With Janet I learned how to be a mother, and I think a lot of what I learned from her about raising children helped me to be a very good teacher.

Things got into a routine, and I took some classes in the mornings and some in the evenings. We three adults changed diapers, fed the kids, took them to the park, played with them, talked with them, sang to them, bathed them, told them stories, got them into their pajamas, and put them to bed. I was amazed to see how much my brother participated in everything about the children. He was not as patient as Janet but he was a very good father. Personally I think that if he had not been a father so early in life and in his career, he would not have survived the way he has. He and Janet took their children with them wherever they went for jobs. How many parents do that? Martin loved being a father. He needed to be a father although at times I know the responsibility was frightening for him. Soon Emilio and

Ramon made some room for Charlie. Charlie was very little when the family went on tour with *The Subject Was Roses*. They returned to New York and soon Renée was born.

Getting Involved

The Civil Rights Movement was on everyone's mind in the 1960s because of the civil unrest and protests leading up to the passage of the Civil Rights Act in 1964. This act declared that segregation because of race, color, sex, religion, or country of origin was illegal. Martin Luther King, Jr., Robert Kennedy, and others continued their efforts to promote desegregation and respect across the country in the years that followed. Inspired by these people, Martin spoke to the theater manager where *The Subject Was Roses* was playing and floated the idea to have a performance to benefit the Civil Rights Movement. The manager gave his consent and Martin approached other performers both on and off Broadway to lend their support to the event. Sammy Davis, Jr., Barbra Streisand, and many others attended, making the event very successful. Martin Luther King, Jr. unexpectedly attended the play and was standing alone backstage in the wings. According to Fr. John Dear, one of Martin's closest friends, Martin had a chance to greet him, but suddenly lacked the confidence to approach the great man. Afterwards, when another opportunity arose, he got stuck between two people and never did meet the Rev. King.[8]

Martin writes at length about his admiration for Bobby Kennedy in chapter 2 of *Along the Way*. Since Bobby's days as Attorney General in his brother President John F. Kennedy's administration, especially when he acted to protect the Freedom Riders in 1961, Martin had been impressed and considered him "a decent, honest, hopeful man with enormous compassion and humanity."[9] Martin volunteered for his New

York State senate campaign in 1964, and on October 4 of that year, just before the election, several actors were asked to attend a rally to show their support for Bobby's campaign. The rally was to oppose the closing of the Brooklyn Navy Yard, and Martin agreed only if he could meet Bobby. He sat directly in front of Martin and Janet, and at the urging of an aid, he turned to greet them.[10]

Some of the few words Bobby spoke at that event stayed with Martin: "I think what should guide all of us is not the fact that the struggle is so difficult, but what should really guide us is what George Bernard Shaw once said, 'Some men see things as they are and say, Why? I dream of things that never were and say, Why not?' "[11]

Three of Martin's heroes were assassinated in the 1960s: John F. Kennedy in 1963 and both Martin Luther King, Jr. and Robert F. Kennedy in 1968. Their efforts to uplift humanity influenced Martin greatly, and his desire for human rights and justice, evidenced in his early life, was growing. The day after Martin Luther King, Jr. was killed, on April 5, 1968, Martin recalls hearing more inspiring words that Bobby told a crowd in Cleveland, Ohio: "Whenever we tear at the fabric of life which another man has painfully and clumsily woven for himself and his children the whole nation is degraded."

Martin follows with a reflection on the word *clumsily* and why he became an actor:

> It's a beautiful sentence because it is so true. We never know in advance what our next step will be. We just take a step, even if it is a clumsy, stumbling one. Sometimes we have to admit, "That wasn't a very good move, I'll try this instead." Or "Oops, I didn't realize how expensive that was going to be." Or, "Oh, dear, I didn't realize that you loved me." But through it all we keep walking. We keep living. I didn't become an actor because I was organized to be one.

I became an actor because of my clumsy attempt to become myself. We, all of us, just keep engaging in these clumsy attempts to realize ourselves. It's such a perfect expression of what it is to be human.[12]

In 1974 Martin would play Attorney General Robert F. Kennedy to William Devane's President Kennedy in the made-for-television docudrama about the Cuban missile crisis, *The Missiles of October*. Writer Stanley R. Greenburg won a Humanitas Prize[13] for the script.

Martin played a US president for the first time in 1984 in the television miniseries *Kennedy*. Martin was nominated for a Golden Globe and won a British Academy of Film and Television Arts (BAFTA) award for his performance as John F. Kennedy. In 2006 the film *Bobby* was released. It was written and directed by Martin's son Emilio and is a cinematic imagining of people's lives in the hours leading up to the assassination of Robert F. Kennedy at the Ambassador Hotel in Los Angeles on June 4, 1968. The film is an homage to the era and to RFK's memory, with an impressive ensemble cast that also includes both Martin and Emilio.

Martin serves on the board of directors of the Robert F. Kennedy Center for Justice and Human Rights and has taken part in the center's activities, such as "Speak Truth to Power." The center is important to Martin because of its aims: "The RFK Center strives to achieve Robert F. Kennedy's vision of a just and peaceful world by partnering with human rights leaders, teaching social justice, and advancing corporate responsibility."

The Incident in 1967 was Martin's first film role. He played one of two thugs who terrorize subway riders in New York. That same year Martin was asked to reprise his role for the film version of *The Subject Was Roses*, released in 1968. He was nominated for a Golden Globe for his performance.

A chance for the family to leave New York came when Martin was signed on to act in Mike Nichols's film adaptation of Joseph Heller's satirical antiwar novel *Catch 22* in 1969. Filming was to begin in Mexico and move on to Los Angeles and Rome.

While in Mexico the family decided not to live in a hotel as other cast members and crew were doing. For financial reasons they rented a small house in a local neighborhood, and Emilio and Ramon briefly attended the nearby Catholic school. After a couple of months in Mexico, the family rented a house in Los Angeles. The children adapted well to southern California but Martin needed to go to Rome to shoot some scenes for *Catch 22*. Rather than take the whole family for a couple of months, he took Emilio, then seven, and Ramon, five, with him. They made a memorable side trip to Parderrubias, Spain, Pop's hometown.

Martin and the boys stayed with Pop's youngest brother, Matías, and his wife Juaquina, in what had been the family home, at least since his grandfather's time. Pop's brother Lorenzo lived there as well. Martin and his sons slept in the room and the very bed where Martin's father was born. And there on the wall was the poster of *The Subject Was Roses* that Martin had given Pop in New York, along with pictures and newspaper clippings of Martin over the years. Finally, he had the reassurance and recognition he had so longed for from Pop. (Carmen has that poster today at her home in Madrid.)

By the time *Catch 22* was released in 1970, Martin had begun acting in a string of made-for-television movies, or movies of the week, such as *Goodbye, Raggedy Ann,* and *Mongo's Back in Town.*

Badlands to Hollywood

In 1972 a young director named Terrence Malick signed Martin and an unknown actress named Sissy Spacek in one of her first motion picture roles, *Badlands*. The story, though fictionalized, is based on two real-life teen murderers, Charles Starweather and his girlfriend, Caril Ann Fugate, who went on a killing spree in 1958. Martin drew on his inner James Dean,[14] an actor he had always admired, for the attitude, mannerisms, and look of a restless young drifter, Kit Caruthers. When Kit, a twenty-five-year-old psychopath, loses his job as a small town Nebraska garbage man, he runs off with a fifteen-year-old girl, Holly, after he kills her father. Emilio and Charlie both made their film debuts in *Badlands* as "two boys playing under a lamppost."[15]

Emilio remembers that after auditioning and being offered the role in *Badlands*, his dad realized this was the chance of a lifetime: "My dad pulled over to the side of the road in his car and started weeping because someone had faith enough in him to give him this chance."[16] Martin told *The Guardian* newspaper in 1999 that *Badlands* was the best script he had ever read. "It was mesmerizing. It disarmed you. It was a period piece, and yet of all time. It was extremely American, it caught the spirit of the people, of the culture, in a way that was immediately identifiable. . . . I will never be better than I was in *Badlands*."[17] *Badlands* premiered at the 1973 New York Film Festival and twenty years later it was placed on the National Film Registry of the Library of Congress as one of America's "culturally, historically, or aesthetically significant films."

Martin's work often took him to distant places, and Janet and the children would accompany him. In 1973 Martin took his family with him to Ireland to film *Catholics*, an episode of *Playhouse 90*. To keep the kids busy Martin bought them a cheap Super 8 movie camera. When they got back home they began making their own movies that would include friends and neighbors who went on to build significant Hollywood careers, such as Rob and Chad Lowe, Diane Lane, Tom Cruise, and Sean Penn.[18]

In 1974 Martin had key roles in two made-for-television movies, *The Execution of Private Slovik*, based on a true story of the only soldier executed for desertion since the Civil War, and *The Missiles of October*. For Martin's brother John, *The Execution of Private Slovik* remains his favorite of all Martin's performances.

To outsiders the early '70s were good years for Martin's career, and in 1974 Martin and Janet moved their family into a ranch-style home in Malibu, California, about an hour's drive from all the Hollywood studios and where they still live today. But Martin's life was fragmenting before his very eyes, and soon all the world would know.

CHAPTER THREE

Spiritual Journey

Saint John of the Cross (1542–91), Carmelite priest, Doctor of the Church, and mystic, is the author of a poem entitled "The Dark Night of the Soul," in Spanish *La noche oscura del alma*. It is about a person's journey to God and the conflicts, stumbles, and falls along the way. The poem is divided into two stages or parts, the purification of the senses and the purification of the spirit, and it could be a map of Martin's life. By the mid-1970s Martin was beginning to walk through a dark night of purification of senses and spirit that would last several years and in some ways continues today.

Martin and his brothers grew up in a neighborhood where drinking was a social norm. People drank and got drunk for weddings, funerals, or any reason, and the Estevez siblings all had been arrested during their young adult years for public intoxication or related incidents. Truth be told, Martin and his brothers were hell-raisers. Later, when he had some spending money in New York, he began going to bars. Alcohol was becoming a problem that would almost kill Martin, a problem he would not be able to overcome by himself.

Martin admits that between jobs he would give in to bouts of self-pity and anger and would take refuge in alcohol, even as his family was growing and his career was in full swing. It is remarkable that, in the midst of his inner chaos and busy professional schedule, Martin was about to begin making television dramas and films for a Los Angeles-based Catholic production company, Paulist Productions, and he would do so across the span of twenty-five years.

Insight

Father Ellwood "Bud" Kieser, CSP (1929–2000), founder of Paulist Productions, launched an Emmy Award-winning syndicated anthology television series called *Insight* in 1960 that ran until 1984. According to Michael R. Rhodes, who produced and/or directed fifty-two episodes of the series, including several that starred Martin, "Bud believed the purpose of *Insight* was to serve God by serving man's search for meaning, freedom, and love" and that both men were "fellow travelers on their journeys of faith."

Martin's work for the *Insight* series was on network television, and while some might not consider it "popular television" it is a significant Catholic contribution to mainstream television that lasted almost a quarter of a century.

Rhodes wrote, in the unpublished memoir that he kindly prepared as a reference for this book, that Fr. Bud first asked Martin "in 1970 to star in two episodes of *Insight*. The first was 'Old King Cole,' a story about a man named Cole who lures a bunch of losers into his bar. He promises to fulfill their dreams if they will abdicate their dignity and do his bidding. They all agree, including a junkie played by Martin, until a little blind girl, in love with life, wanders into the bar and confronts its owner. The second episode was 'Chipper,' written by Lan O'Kun. It is a story about a man who drops by to visit his old buddy, the owner of a restaurant, but is met by a stranger, played by Martin, who is dressed as the waiter who serves him his last meal."

Writer Lan O'Kun, who went on to write for *The Love Boat* and *Little House on the Prairie*, said of Martin's performance in "Chipper," "Martin was beautiful."

In 1971 Martin starred in "Death of an Elephant," written by Jack Hanrahan, where an Irish wake triggers some strange revelations among the mourners. Then came "The Clown of Freedom" written by Terrance Sweeney. Sweeney had this to say about Martin:

> Over the past four decades, I've had the good fortune of working with many of the finest talents in the entertainment industry. Among the most professionally satisfying and inspiring were collaborations with Martin. I first met him when he starred in an *Insight* script I wrote, "The Clown of Freedom." He played the role of Ramon (Bobo), the leader of a clown troupe who, under threat of death, was ordered by a Central American dictator to orient his humor in favor of the junta. Ramon was the only one of his troupe to refuse, and his execution gave courage to his friends who witnessed his death. During that filming, which was the first *Insight* to be shot outside a studio setting, I witnessed Martin's dedication as an actor, his positive and genial attitude towards his fellow actors, and his passionate dedication to social justice issues. [In hindsight, Martin's role in "The Clown of Freedom" was prophetic, given his future work for peace and justice in Central America.]
>
> Off set, Martin spent a lot of time with Henry Proach, who played one of the actors in Bobo's troupe. He looked wizened, yet wise and laughed a lot. I wondered why Henry and Martin were such good friends and found out later that they met at the Living Theatre in 1960 where Martin

and Henry were fellow actors and janitors. When Martin's career began to flourish, he moved to Los Angeles and helped Henry make the move as well. Over the years Henry became an important part of the Estevez family. He played roles in films with them including a number of parts in Paulist films. Emilio dedicated his 1986 movie *Wisdom* to Henry, an actor who played all of his roles in life and the movies with commitment and heart.

After "The Clown of Freedom" came "Roommates on a Rainy Day" (1973), a sensitive exploration of the meaning of commitment; "The Crime of Innocence" (1974) about a neighborhood that becomes frightened when a group of mentally ill teens and their director move in; and "When the Walls Came Tumblin' Down" (1974), a "wonderful fantasy about God who gives an aging tailor the gift of understanding."

Rhodes recalls a 1978 *Insight* episode that made him think of Martin's experience filming *Apocalypse Now* in the Philippines: "'Just before Eve' was also written by Lan O'Kun and focused on a man named Adam, played by Martin, who is bored and lonely, roaming the Garden of Eden alone and unhappy when God challenges him to seek the cause of his distress. It made me think of Martin's own distress in the Philippines and the love and support he received from his family."

In 1978 Martin starred in "Is Anyone Listening," written by John McGreevey (1922–2010). Martin plays a soul-searching priest, Father Tom, who is undergoing therapy. He asks, "Who am I?" as he painfully explores his role as the "perfect priest." This episode, made after Martin's heart attack in the Philippines while filming *Apocalypse Now* and while he was still on his personal journey back to the church and the practice of faith, is currently on YouTube. While it has the look of a soap opera and the music is rather melo-dramatic, the human story and struggle is real enough, and the performances by all the actors are quite good.

Rhodes also recalls how Emilio began his acting career:

In 1979 Emilio cowrote, directed, and starred in a Santa Monica High School play about Vietnam veterans called *Echoes of an Era* and invited his parents to watch it. Martin was fascinated by his son's performance, and "began to realize: my God, he's one of us." Martin wanted his son to begin his professional acting career with a producer he could trust, and asked Bud if he would consider Emilio for a part. Emilio was cast in a small part in *A Long Road Home* (1980), an *Insight* episode also written by Lan O'Kun. I think it must have been great for Emilio to perform with his father.

Martin won an Emmy for Outstanding Individual Achievement in Religious Programing for this episode in 1981, the year Martin would return to the practice of his faith. Rhodes went on to work with Emilio in several more productions for the Paulists, including *Tex* (1982), an adaptation of S.E. Hinton's 1979 novel.

Martin continued to donate his time and talent in Paulist Productions' first prime-time network television movie, *The Fourth Wise Man* (1985). Tom Fontana wrote the script, and I produced it. It starred Martin as the fourth wise man, and Alan Arkin as his servant. Martin's character, which never quite caught up with the other three kings, finds his own king in his own way. Nearly all of the members of the Arkin and Estevez families had roles in the movie. It was lots of fun and was very successful.

Years later, because of his personal respect for Dorothy Day (1897–1980), Martin played a lead role in the 1996

Paulist feature film *Entertaining Angels: The Dorothy Day Story*. John Wells wrote the script and this time I directed. Martin played Peter Maurin (1877–1949), Dorothy's spiritual mentor and cofounder of the Catholic Worker. The film tells the story of Dorothy's evolution from political radical to her conversion to Catholicism and the hardships and joy she experienced on the journey. She not only worked tirelessly for the poor and unloved; she lived among them and considered herself to be one of them.

Rhodes said that over the years they worked together "Martin's relationship with Bud (as his friends called him) was both spiritual and tumultuous. But Bud never let his friendship with Martin go cold and neither did Martin. No matter what their disagreements, Martin always accepted Bud's invitation to play a role in another *Insight* episode or a Paulist produced film, unless he had a conflict involving the needs of his family, was taking a stand for social justice, or had a movie contract he couldn't break. . . . Both Martin and Bud dived deep into life, searching for God in everyone, everywhere."[1]

Martin says about his collaboration with Fr. Kieser, "He had a mission to spread the gospel in a nonreligious but spiritual way that resonated with anyone watching. He was very hard to say 'no' to. In fact, you couldn't say 'no,' you had to make room for his projects because you realized it was for your own good. It was not a career move," Martin said with a smile in his voice, "but a growth move."

But even working with Fr. Bud Kieser in the 1970s didn't get Martin back to the sacraments.

When a Father Dies

In 1973 Pop suffered a heart attack and died the following year. Martin went to see his father about six weeks before his death and did not expect him to die so suddenly. He describes Pop's death as a "grave shock." Carmen writes:

> The last time I saw Pop was in the hospital in the summer of 1974. My partner, Angel, had come with me from Spain because I wanted him to meet my father, and I wanted Pop to know that even though I was not married, I had a stable relationship with a very good man. He was surrounded by about half of his children that day, and we were being quite noisy. A nurse came in and asked us to try to quiet down. I asked her if we were causing Pop any problems. Should we leave him alone to rest? No, she said. He was better than ever but there were other patients nearby who would be bothered by the loud noise. We continued our visit with Pop but we kept our voices down.
>
> The last words I remember from Pop were in Spanish. He told me that his children were his greatest *tesoro* (treasure). I laughed and reminded Pop that all our lives he had called us mugs and hooligans, troublemakers and fools, dummies and know-it-alls, etc. "And now you call us your treasure?" He smiled and repeated, *Mi tesoro mas grande* (my greatest treasure). He was very calm and had said earlier that day that when he had seen all his children one more time, he would die peacefully. That was in August, and all his children did come to visit him before the summer was over and he died on October 26 of that year.

Martin's brothers went to Pop's funeral in Dayton but Martin headed to Madrid to be with his sister Carmen, who had become very ill.

"We see now as in a mirror" (1 Cor 13:12)

When Paul wrote to the Corinthians about love and the maturity of faith, he could have been speaking into the future to Martin. He was about to look into a mirror and break it, and in the shattered reflection of himself, through the haze of alcohol, God was there, however dimly Martin would be able to see.

In 1976 director Francis Ford Coppola was looking for an actor to replace Harvey Keitel, whom Coppola had fired, to play in his film about the Vietnam War, *Apocalypse Now*. Martin and his entire family were in Rome where he was filming *The Cassandra Crossing* when he got a phone call asking him to fly to Los Angeles immediately and meet with Coppola. Martin was offered the role the day after an extremely brief meeting with Coppola at the airport. Martin flew back to Rome on Easter Sunday, completed *The Cassandra Crossing* on Monday, and departed for the Philippines on Tuesday to begin filming Coppola's movie. The making of this film remains arguably one of the most difficult in cinema history, as documented in the film *Hearts of Darkness: A Filmmaker's Apocalypse*, created from source footage shot by Eleanor Coppola, Francis's wife. It debuted at Cannes in 1991.

For Martin, making this film became a personal apocalypse. He played the central character of the story, Captain Willard Scott, in a cinematic epic that is primarily an adaptation of Joseph Conrad's 1899 novella *Heart of Darkness*. Scott is tasked with tracking down and killing a renegade Green Berets officer named Kurtz, played by Marlon Brando. (It's ironic that Joseph Conrad was one of Mary Ann Estevez's favorite authors.)

Martin is often asked if this film is one of his favorites, and while he knows the film made him a star that audiences around the world would recognize, he explains, "I relate films to the experience of making them and *Apocalypse Now* was not a happy experience. I was so fragmented and making the film was a fragmenting experience. I did not have a center. I was an actor one day and a father and a husband the next," because his family was with him.

It was desperately hot in the Philippine jungle and Martin, as the main character, was in almost every scene. Less than two months into production, Hurricane Olga hit the Philippines and destroyed the sets for the film. Production was halted for two months while the sets were rebuilt. Martin and his family headed back to Malibu. Once home, Martin struggled with having to return to the dense jungle to finish the film. He dreaded the thought of spending so much time filming in a small patrol boat on a river. Further, it was a perilous situation for him because he could not swim. When he could not avoid going back he actually took swimming lessons as a precaution in case of an accident. The family returned to the Philippines for what they hoped would be a brief stay.

Emilio began noticing his father's issues with alcohol a few years before, and now Martin was drinking a lot and smoking up to three packs of cigarettes a day, eating mostly junk food, and losing weight. Emilio, then fourteen, wanted to go home more than anything. He was starting to drink beer and hang out in bars, a time in his life he writes about extensively in chapter 9 of *Along the Way*. After a heated battle with his father, Emilio got his wish, and he and Ramon were sent back to Malibu. The younger children stayed in the Philippines with their parents. The stress of family, career, the intensity of making the film, personal demons such as guilt and lack of confidence, along with Coppola's constant script rewrites and grueling schedule, took their toll on Martin.

On Friday evening, March 4, with Janet away in Manila, Martin began experiencing chest pains. The next day he had a heart attack and nervous breakdown at the same time. He crawled from his room and along the road on his hands and knees to the wardrobe trailer and got help. The fist thing he did was to ask for a priest. Martin received the sacrament of anointing, or as known in popular parlance, the last rites.

He was taken by helicopter to the hospital where he wept continually. Janet stayed with him for the six weeks he was in the hospital, sometimes sleeping on the floor beside his bed. While healing from the coronary, Janet arranged for Martin to speak to a therapist in New York via phone, hoping to heal mind and body together, at least for the time being.

The opening scenes of *Apocalypse Now* show Martin as a deeply conflicted and very drunk Captain Scott fighting off his demons in a steaming Saigon hotel room in the middle of a war. It's a brilliant scene that shows externally the internal reality of what the total breakdown of a man looks like, a man whose conscience is so wounded that he can only drink himself into oblivion. Martin was extremely intoxicated when it came time to begin shooting that scene. Coppola knew and let the camera roll, at Martin's insistence, on one of the most despairing unscripted scenes ever shot. Martin said about the experience:

> I was 36 years old, and I was an alcoholic. . . . The sequence was in large part reflection of my own personal brokenness. I was not a practicing Catholic at the time, and I had no clue what I was getting into with the film. I had been called in to replace someone [Harvey Keitel] and I came into a volatile situation [on the set]. Six weeks after I arrived in the Philippines Hurricane Olga hit and the film was delayed. A year later I had a heart attack, a really close call.
>
> In film, if something is impersonal, no one cares. Things that last are things that cost people and the actors that portray them. I had an instinct that I could endure this role

if I could be honest. I was playing a frightened, confused professional killer [Capt. Benjamin Willard], an unstable frightened alcoholic. I didn't have a clue who this character was supposed to be and the director [Francis Ford Coppola] said to me: "It's you. Whoever wants to arrive at any kind of certainty as an actor brings themselves." I realized I could wrestle this demon. There's an old saying that an artist gets a license to play this part. I used the license to go to a place that was both cathartic and terrifying. My poor wife, Janet, got a glimpse of this poor devil in that sequence, the anger, fear, resentment, and disappointment that had built up over 36 years. It was filmed on my 36th birthday.[2]

In a taped interview in 1982 about the opening sequence in *Apocalypse Now*, Martin talked to filmmaker Emile de Antonio, who would later direct him in *In the King of Prussia*:

That was shot on my thirty-sixth birthday, August 3, 1976. Frankly, I was intoxicated; I had been drinking all day. I'd lived in that room for a couple of days. Day and night. I had no business being on screen. Francis didn't want me to do it, but I insisted. I said "There is something here I need to investigate." He put two cameras up and said, "Whenever you want to quit, just say it." He was very compassionate, very sweet, and at the same time protective. He asked, "What is it you want to do?" I said I didn't know, and he said, "I'll go along with that. Fine. OK." I was a raving lunatic. Joe Lowery, a Vietnam veteran and friend, was teaching me hand-to-hand karate and judo. He explained that the best way to train when by yourself is in front of a mirror, because nothing is faster than your own reflection. I was in front of a mirror. I made a chop; I was too close; I hit it and cut myself and Francis yelled, "Cut!" And I said, "No, Keep rolling." And he said, "No, you're bleeding," and I said, "Yes, I know, let's go on; I'm not hurt, I want to explore this." He held the footage in the Philippines for a long time. He finally said, "You must see this footage. I don't want to use it unless you see it." And I said, "No, I can't look at it; it's a part of myself I'm not able to look at; I'm not able to deal with it." Francis said, "I don't want you to be surprised or embarrassed." I said, "Look, we're dealing with a guy here who's in a very bad way. This could be useful to the film." He offered to show it to me after he cut it, but I refused. The first time I ever saw it was in the theater.[3]

The film was running way behind schedule and over budget, and Coppola was having his own struggles, most notably with funding and an unprepared and recalcitrant Marlon Brando. Coppola flew in Joe Estevez, Martin's youngest brother and an actor with his own severe drinking problem,[4] to stand in for Martin in some scenes and later, during editing, to do some of the voice-over work because Martin was then busy on other projects. Frank and John Estevez, their brothers, can easily identify the scenes that Joe appears in, though to the public it is almost impossible to tell the difference. Joe did not receive credit for his screen work in *Apocalypse Now*, something that still bothers him.

After six weeks convalescence Martin returned to the set and the film wrapped about eight weeks later. It took almost three years to edit the film. It opened in 1979 to mixed reviews but was extremely successful at the box office.

Martin's performance won him an Oscar nomination for Best Actor; the film was nominated for nine Academy Awards all together. As usual, however, Martin asked that his name be removed from consideration due to his insistence that the performing arts are invariably team efforts. The film also made him an internationally recognized star.

With the heart attack, the nervous breakdown, and what he called a near death experience, Martin found himself in a dark night, deeply. The purification of his senses and spirit intensified.

In November 2007, *Hearts of Darkness: A Filmmaker's Apocalypse* was released on DVD. Martin recounts:

> When it came out I had a new assistant who didn't know me very well. The film is very shocking and an honest portrayal of what went down during production. So she was watching it with me and she said to me, "This must be very upsetting for you." I replied, "It's not who I am now but who I was." I am conscious of being different from that time. The journey was made in terrible increments, it was hard to reveal myself and I saw it in a flash while watching the documentary—and saw that I had moved on. I saw where I used to be when the film was made . . .

For about three years following *Apocalypse Now*, Martin continued to drink heavily and even separated from his family a couple of times. One night in San Francisco someone stole a large sum of money from his wallet. He was very drunk, caused a huge ruckus, and ended up in jail for the night for hitting a policeman. His alcoholism and behavior affected his children. They continued in school, however. Charlie was getting into baseball, Ramon into dance and performance, and Emilio was developing his own skills as an actor in Santa Monica High School. Renee liked reading, writing, and horses. Martin briefly returned to the practice of his faith but he didn't keep it up. He let his image of an angry and punishing God get in the way.

He kept working, however, and completed three more *Insight* episodes for Paulist Productions. His final *Insight* episode, "A Long Road Home," aired in 1980.

Martin and Fr. Bud remained friends until the priest's last days in 2000. Father Frank Desiderio, CSP, Fr. Kieser's successor as head of Paulist Productions, remembers:

> Martin came to see Bud every night at Cedars Sinai Hospital in Los Angeles for his last few days. I don't remember exactly how many days it was but I think it was about four. Bud had come home from the cancer surgery but then his body threw off a blood clot, which went to his brain, which is what killed him. He was in a coma for those days.
>
> Martin would visit each evening. He would visit with whoever was there; different people every night. Each evening, just before we left, I would lead the group in prayer. I'd use the night prayer of the church as a loose model. Martin was very much involved in the prayer, doing readings, offering spontaneous petitions, and to close out the prayer Martin would lead whoever was there in singing. One of the songs was *Amazing Grace*. He was convinced that Bud could hear us, even if he wasn't responsive.
>
> Emilio Estevez, Martin's son, also came to see Bud and brought him a portable CD player and some CDs of music to listen to, spirituals and classical, if I remember correctly. Emilio put the headphones on Bud and adjusted the volume, hoping the music, which Bud loved, would bring him some comfort.
>
> One evening, after we left Bud's room, Martin and I and a few others went to dinner across the street at Jerry's Deli (which is now closed). This was during Martin's days starring in *The West Wing* (1999—2006). People were very good about not disturbing him during his meal, but as we were leaving they approached him at the door asking for autographs. He was always very gracious.

Martin was nominated for an Emmy for *Blind Ambition*, a 1979 CBS docudrama about the Watergate scandal and subsequent cover-up. Martin played John Dean, White House Counsel during the Nixon years, a man who played a key role in the events that brought down a US president. Again, Martin asked that his name be withdrawn from award consideration.

Gandhi

In 1980 Sir Richard Attenborough, the British director, asked Martin to play the role of an American journalist, Walker, in his epic film *Gandhi*. The film chronicles the life of the Mohandas K. Gandhi (played by Ben Kingsley), who started off life in South Africa in 1869 and was assassinated in India in 1948. Gandhi led the independence movement in India and advocated nonviolence and fasting as means to obtain social and political change. In the film, Walker comes to believe in Gandhi's nonviolent philosophy of activism.

Martin hesitated to take the role because his personal life was still not in a good place, but he did anyway. Now eighteen, Emilio accompanied his father to India for the filming. Although Martin's role in the film was relatively small, Attenborough hired Emilio as a stand in for Martin. Encountering Gandhi's worldview impressed Martin greatly at this seminal time in his life. The poverty of India, the condition of the children, and the pervasiveness of death at every turn, stunned Martin and made him grateful for his own life and family. "The experience in India was the one I really needed. That was the final step that pushed me toward coming to grips with my spirituality . . . [and] really solidified the journey for me. I had to surrender to my need. And rather than coming to the church out of fear, I came out of love."[5] He donated his entire earnings from *Gandhi* to charity.

In *Along the Way*[6] Martin tells about the many ways that the experience in India changed him and improved his relationship with Emilio. Martin already knew about Mother Teresa and her work when an opportunity arose for him and Emilio to meet her during the filming of *Gandhi*. She and Richard Attenborough had become friends, and he invited some of the people on the film to go to Calcutta for Mass at the Home for Dying, where they would meet Mother Teresa afterward. Martin was very excited about going but Emilio kept questioning him about his motivations to meet Mother Teresa. As Martin raved about how famous she was for her work with the poor, he realized that he wanted to meet her so he could brag about it. Martin decided not to go to Calcutta. It was then, he writes, that he realized his son had become a teacher to him. It would be ten years before he would meet Mother Teresa and during those years her life and work for humanity continued to impress Martin profoundly. Martin attributes the time that he and Emilio spent together in India as a time of "self-discovery" that "cemented a relationship of mutual respect and real love and support between us . . . that continues to this day."[7]

Martin admits that when he learned about Gandhi's life and marriage and the vows that Gandhi and his wife took, he came to realize that marriage meant "an end to selfishness." He reflected on his own marriage and resolved to make "serious adjustments" as he continued to travel his spiritual journey.[8] When Martin and Janet celebrated their fiftieth wedding anniversary in 2011, he said:

> "Janet's the only truly honest person. She tells you the truth, the whole truth, nothing but the truth, all the time." About how their marriage lasted this long in Hollywood, he said "Honest to God, I don't know. I adore her. I didn't get to know her until we were married twenty years. I didn't realize what she was doing. She was always smarter with me. She didn't hit me over the head with it. She just sort of

waited for me to mature a little bit. I don't have a clue who she is. I really don't. I know who she was at that time or this time. She's always, always ahead of me. With the greatest heart. And the most sensible person. So consistent. So absolutely, totally consistent every day of her life. And extremely funny. She'll have you laughing. Really, you'll be falling down laughing."[9]

Father John Dear, a friend to both Martin and Janet for more than thirty years, says that "Janet is a faithful, loving wife and that they are utterly devoted to one another."

The experience of making *Apocalypse Now* and his physical and mental breakdown, then making *Gandhi*, was bringing Martin closer to a definitive return to the Catholic church, the anchor of his faith and humanity.

Catharsis

In an interview with Martin in 2011 for the *National Catholic Reporter*, Martin talked about his return to faith:

> *Apocalypse Now* began a journey for me that culminated in Paris in 1981. This is when I was able to bring it all together—my life, my family, my career, my brokenness. I was doing this little film in Paris and the family couldn't come because of school and things. I had time to walk around and reflect on all that had gone down before, and I ran into Terrence Malick. I had known him from the early '70s, since *Badlands*. At that time, in 1981, he was living under the radar. He is an articulate and spiritual man, an Episcopalian, and he became a kind of spiritual adviser for me. We would talk endlessly when I wasn't working. We would talk about spirituality and philosophy and the journey.
>
> Malick also became a kind of life coach for me. He became a great anchor for me. The last book he gave me to

read, and he had me read it several times, was Dostoyevsky's 1880 masterpiece, *The Brothers Karamazov*, and it transformed my spirit. When I finished reading it I put it down and literally got up and walked to St. Joseph Church, the English-speaking parish in Paris. It was May Day, a holiday in France, so I had the day off and I banged on the door and this Irish Passionist priest opened the door and said, "What's going on?" I told him, "I have been away from the church for a long time and I'd like to go to confession." He made an appointment to meet with me the next day, and I have never looked back.

I had dropped in at St. Joseph's occasionally while in Paris, so I was not unfamiliar. But I was fascinated by the new Mass. I had been aware of changes but I had not been practicing for such a long time. I hadn't wanted to rejoin the church and come back to a sense of fear and condemnation that I had absorbed growing up, that God would strike me down. When I had the heart attack I got the Anointing of the Sick in the hospital. I had a great fear of dying and going to hell. But the thing is, I loved the church as a boy.[10]

With his return, or reversion, to the practice of his Catholic faith, meaningful lessons and experiences began to coalesce to further shape Martin's spirituality. He experienced an inner freedom, and his gifts as a person began to emerge and transcend his acting. He rededicated himself to his marriage and family. He had learned about fairness from his mother, and his teenaged efforts as a caddy to demand a just wage, not only for himself—but for all the caddies— manifested an innate sense of community and justice. His impulses to help the poor as a young actor and to promote civil rights were evidence of a deep-seated generosity that now (2014), thirty-five years after his reversion to faith, are more mature and as strong as ever.

Martin also grew in self-knowledge in these years. He realized:

> There is this terrible thing in our profession, about the desperate need to be loved, liked, recognized. Maybe we didn't get it in our families, or we think we deserve more. Maybe it's an ego thing. . . . It's about the need for community and the closest thing I could get to community was a play, because you become very close to actors in a play or a film. It is intense and your foibles and vulnerabilities, your behavior, your fears and anxieties are all exposed. But you become community for that very intense time, and people come to know you, really know you, in that very short time. The making of *Apocalypse Now* was not a pleasant time for me but I made some relationships that were and are invaluable to me, Joe Lowry (a Vietnam vet who taught me martial arts) comes to mind.

And he got sober.

Martin explains that he admires Alcoholics Anonymous (AA) because it is a program that reflects Catholic spirituality and this truly resonates with him. He has been a member of the program for more than thirty years. Although it is supposed to be anonymous, Martin says, "the only real people who are anonymous members are doctors and airplane pilots. Once a celebrity mentions AA, it's no longer a secret. Anyway, someone told me about AA after I was sober, and I joined so that I could learn the Twelve Steps and share this with family members."

AA was cofounded by Bill W. Wilson (1895–1971) and Dr. Bob Smith (1879–1950) and influenced by a Catholic nun, Sister Ignatia Gavin, CSA (1889–1966) and Fr. Edward Dowling, SJ (1898–1960.)[11] Martin knows what the program can mean to Catholics: "The Twelve Steps includes practices found in Catholic spirituality: to make a fearless inventory (it is equal to the examination of conscience), to tell it to another person is like confession or reconciliation, and to make amends is like penance and restitution."

Martin explains that it is through the idea of community that he became sober as well as through the church, the sacraments, and participation at Mass: "I knew I needed community, a focus, and I needed Catholicism. It was the only thing that made any sense at all. The mystery of Catholicism still grabs me. Coming back at this point wasn't about fear, but about commitment and love, sharing your life experiences, living for one another—this is the only thing that made sense to me. Coming as it did in 1981, it was just a matter of time before I would start to become socially active."

And then Martin, with a smile, quotes a friend of his as saying, "The only two things of value that the United States has exported to the world for free are jazz and AA."

CHAPTER FOUR

A Catholic Activist

Now sober, Martin's faith, rekindled by Mass and the sacraments, was maturing. In 1981, when he met the brothers Daniel Berrigan, SJ, and Philip Berrigan (1923–2002), a former Catholic priest and member of the Society of St. Joseph, on the set of the film *In the King of Prussia*, the pieces of Martin's fragmented life seemed to come closer together and to take on fuller purpose.

The film, written and directed by Emile de Antonio (1919–89), details the trial of the brothers and six others who came to be known as the Plowshares Eight. The group had effectively begun the antinuclear, pacifist "beating swords into plowshares" (Isa 2:3-4) Plowshares Movement when they trespassed onto the General Electric Nuclear Missile campus in King of Prussia, Pennsylvania, on September 9, 1980, damaged nose cones on nuclear warheads, and poured blood onto files and papers. They were arrested on many felony and misdemeanor counts.

For their actual trial in early 1981, Montgomery County Judge Samuel Salus II refused to allow the court proceedings to be filmed. After the trial, Daniel Berrigan and Philip

Berrigan asked filmmaker Emile de Antonio to reconstruct the trial from court records.

De Antonio's filmography consists of documentaries that challenged US politics, from McCarthyism to Vietnam to Watergate. He already knew Daniel Berrigan since he had interviewed him for his Oscar-nominated 1969 documentary *In the Year of the Pig,* a film that *New York Times* reviewer Howard Thompson called "a stinging, graphic and often frighteningly penetrating movie"[1] of the then ongoing Vietnam War.

De Antonio hired Martin to play the tough Judge Salus, while the key defendants played themselves: Daniel Berrigan, Philip Berrigan, Sr. Anne Montgomery, Elmer Maas, Molly Rush, Dean Hammer, Fr. Carl Kabat, and John Schuchardt. It was July and it was hot. The set courtroom was constructed in a church on Manhattan's West Side around midtown. It became Martin's classroom on peace, peaceful resistance, and nonviolent joyful protest against war, nuclear armament, and the promotion of human rights from a Catholic perspective.

De Antonio shot the film on videotape in less than forty-eight hours. He later converted the video to 35mm film. *In the King of Prussia* received a grand prize from the International Catholic Organization for Cinema (OCIC) jury at the Ghent Film Festival in 1983. That same year it was screened out of competition at the Berlin Film Festival and received a commendation, again from the OCIC jury, that read "This film is a plea for the critical examination of official information about nuclear weapons and also a test of the moral principles of the audience."[2]

The timing for this film was particularly challenging for Martin, because his brother Mike had just died. Mike was a gay man and former marine who had once considered a pro-golf career. After working in management for a major department store chains and moving from city to city, he studied engineering but finally earned a degree in social work in California. He spent the final years of his life there as a counselor at the Salvation Army.

Martin recalls how he met Daniel Berrigan and describes that moments that can change your life can seem small but prove to be deeply meaningful:

> I had only recently returned to the church, and my second eldest brother, Mike, who was living out here in California, was going through a very difficult time physically. He'd had one leg amputated due to a rare blood-clotting disorder, and he was constantly in and out of hospitals. He was standing right over there, on that porch, and he knew I'd come back to the church, and he was so happy. That was the last time I saw him before he died on July 12, 1981. Mike was one of my heroes; you would have loved this guy. Of all my brothers, Mike had had the most difficult time. Manuel was the favored son and so a lot of the work and looking after the younger kids fell to Mike. He and Pop fought all the time. He finished high school at sixteen, lied about his age, and joined the marines. He was on the way to Korea when he got the news that our mother had died.
>
> I called de Antonio and asked if they would wait for the funeral and he agreed. My brother Al and I went to the funeral home to make arrangements for Mike. We buried him in a simple shroud and a closed casket at Holy Cross Cemetery in Culver City, California.
>
> When we were selecting a memorial card for Mike, the funeral director showed us a sample. It was of a young Asian boy, maybe nineteen or twenty. I asked what had happened, and the director said that he had not been doing well at college and thought he had embarrassed his family and committed suicide. The story touched me.

I kept the memorial card of the Asian boy and when I was on the bench playing the judge there was a break in the proceedings. Dan Berrigan came up to me and introduced himself. He said he was thrilled to meet me. He also told me that now I was part of the nonviolent protest movement over nuclear arms, too. He opened the Bible that was on the bench, and he found the memorial card for the Asian boy that I had placed there. "Who is this? He's just a kid," Berrigan observed, and he promised to pray for him. That was my introduction to Daniel Berrigan.

From that moment on Martin and Dan and Philip became friends. Martin said with that meeting "it was only a matter of time before I would start to become socially active and the Berrigans were responsible for that."

During that same year Martin became involved in human rights in Latin America when he took out an ad in *Daily Variety* and *The Hollywood Reporter* supporting fellow actor Ed Asner's criticism of US involvement in the human rights violations being carried out by the El Salvador government during the 1979–92 war. Ed and Martin had worked together on an episode of *FBI* in 1967 and since then they have joined together many times in support of human rights at home and abroad. This included opposition to the merger of the two actors unions, the Screen Actors Guild (SAG) and the American Federation of Television and Radio Artists (AFTRA) over access to royalties and residuals if the merger occurred. With fifteen other actors they filed a lawsuit to block the merger, but it was thrown out in January 2014.[3]

Civil Disobedience

One of the first civil actions Martin engaged in was to join those who were fasting for justice to support the United Farm

Workers at the La Placita Church (Our Lady Queen of the Angels) in downtown Los Angeles in 1984, but 1986 was the pivotal year. It marked the first time Martin was arrested for civil disobedience and the beginning of his involvement with nonviolent protests. It was the first of sixty-six arrests (or sixty-seven, depending on who you ask). At this point his Catholicism was fully activated. He remembers:

In June of 1986, five years after meeting the Berrigans, I was doing *Wall Street* in New York. I had a Friday (the 21st) off so I called Dan and said I would join him, Fr. John Dear, and Fr. Ned Murphy, SJ (1937–2012), to protest at the Riverside Research Institute offices at the McGraw Hill Building on West 42nd Street. The institute held several defense contracts and was upstairs planning Ronald Reagan's Strategic Defense Initiative, popularly known as "Star Wars," so we blocked the entrance to the workers, which is why we were arrested. Ninety-nine percent of us were Catholic Workers, Catholic actors, teachers, and people from Ned Murphy's organization POTS (Part of the Solution).

We were singing hymns, witnessing to each other, telling stories. Because the CBS program *60 Minutes* was doing a story on Dan and Phil, the television journalist Mike Wallace (1918–2012) was there filming, and the New York City police came. New York cops are a different breed, and some of them are wonderful. So this one cop, who knows Dan, comes up and says, "All right everyone! Listen up! Looky here! I'm giving you five minutes! You're on private property, and if you don't start leaving here in five minutes I'll have to start arresting youse!" So Dan says, "Officer, come on! You know you believe in this!" and the cop answered, "Come on, Father, don't do this!" We were all laughing.

The protest was done so joyfully, as a community, with no leadership. We were all talking to each other about what was going on in the world when they hauled us away in a paddy wagon. That was a wonderful retreat being arrested with this community.

I met my lawyer, Joe Cosgrove, in the paddy wagon (there's a picture of that somewhere). We actually had met earlier but I like to say we met in that paddy wagon! Once we were at the station house where they were booking everyone and telling us we had to come back for the trial, Joe came around collecting the summons and telling us what would happen if we didn't show up on the appointed day. I asked him, "Who are you?" He responded that he was a lawyer who had just been arrested with us, and that yes, he was part of the cause, too. Joe is a Notre Dame graduate, and today we are the closest of friends. He defends people who are arrested at protests.

This was the community that I had come into. I realized: It's not about you! You're not going to change the world so don't get any ideas. If you change yourself, you've done it. If you show up and you do it when no one is watching, now you are talking. You do it, these peaceful demonstrations and protests, because you cannot *not* do it. As Dan said, "I cannot *not* do this and be myself."

The *Los Angeles Times* printed a United Press International (UPI) story stating that Martin called the protest and getting arrested "the happiest day of my life."[4]

A Community of Activists

Over the decades, Martin has made a number of close friends in the faith-based movements for justice and peace. They have shared his journey and his passion for peace. At the top of the list are Daniel Berrigan and Philip Berrigan. By 2014, Father Daniel Berrigan was frail and elderly, in his 90s and living in a New York Jesuit infirmary. Philip Berrigan died in 2002. Other activist friends include Phil's wife Elizabeth McAlister of Jonah House, Baltimore, Maryland; Dr. Davida Coady of the Options Recovery Center in Berkeley, California, and cofounder with Martin of the San Carlos Foundation; Joe Cosgrove, a Notre Dame graduate, lawyer, and activist in Wilkes-Barre, Pennsylvania; Fr. Louie Vitale, a Franciscan priest who started the protest movement at the Nevada Test Site; Kerry Kennedy, director of the Robert F. Kennedy Human Rights Center; Roy Bourgeois of the School of the Americas Watch; Catholic Workers such as Jeff Dietrich and Catherine Morris of the Los Angeles Catholic Worker; Kathleen Rumpf; and Fr. John Dear, a long time peace activist and author.

Martin had several other close activist friends who have since died, including Cesar Chavez, founder of the United Farm Workers; Mitch Snyder of the Community for Creative Nonviolence in Washington, DC; Fr. Bill O'Donnell of Berkeley, California; Rev. William Sloane Coffin, former chaplain of Yale and Riverside Church in New York City; and Fr. Ned Murphy, SJ, founder of POTS (Part of the Solution), a homeless shelter in the Bronx.

Father John Dear is the author of thirty books on peace and nonviolence as well as an organizer and lecturer. He was recently nominated for the Nobel Peace Prize by Archbishop Desmond Tutu. A Jesuit for many years, he recently left the Jesuits and joined a diocese in California where he remains a priest and continues to work for peace and justice. Martin wrote the foreword to his 2008 autobiography, *A Persistent Peace*. There John describes meeting Martin in New York City in 1986 while Martin was filming *Wall Street* with his son Charlie and Michael Douglas. A mutual friend, Jack Marth of POTS, introduced John to Martin after they attended a Pax Christi Mass at New York University. John remembers:

We shook hands, and Martin invited us to go for a walk. So we set off and walked the streets of Manhattan all through the night, talking about the movie, the peace movement, our heroes Dan and Phil Berrigan, civil disobedience, Jesus and the gospels, and our hopes for peace. Martin was full of energy and excitement and told me his life story. We've been talking like that ever since. That's the way he is with everyone—full of life, energy, interest, and excitement. His commitment to his faith and his family and the work for peace and justice is extraordinary. He's one of my closest friends, and I can't imagine doing any of this work without him. I'm sure our other friends would say the same thing. I do not know anyone quite as full of life, with such a generous, loving spirit.

I remember hearing, for example, that Cesar Chavez had three framed pictures on his desk—the Sacred Heart of Jesus, the Immaculate Heart of Mary, and Martin! That is the way we all feel about Martin.

Over the decades we have been involved together in a hundred events, trips, and protests. We were arrested together protesting the Riverside Research Institute in New York City, where they studied nuclear weapons; many times at the Nevada nuclear weapons test site near Las Vegas; several times at the federal building in Los Angeles after the six Jesuits were killed in El Salvador on November 16, 1989; at the US Capitol to protest US military aid to El Salvador; many times at the School of the Americas protests in Georgia; and at Lawrence Livermore Laboratories in Livermore, California, along with Rev. William Sloane Coffin, to protest nuclear weapons. In 1994, Martin visited Philip Berrigan and me in jail in North Carolina after our 1993 plowshares disarmament action and even joined the civil disobedience in the courtroom with twenty-five others to protest the judge's decision to ban any discussion of the US military in our trial. He invited me several times to events with Cesar Chavez and later joined Daniel Berrigan and me for Mass and dinner with our community in New York City whenever he was on the east coast.

I remember when I was living in Guatemala in 1991, Martin, Davida, Joe, and Fr. Bill came to visit me for a week, and we traveled together and then went to El Salvador for a week. We met so many struggling people, but continued talking the whole time. I remember he and I spent one entire day sitting in the back of a pickup truck riding through the Salvadoran countryside talking about Gandhi and Jesus.

When I was living and working in Richmond, Virginia, running a large community center for disenfranchised African-American women and children, Martin came and led a very successful fund-raising picnic and event. In 1997, when I was living in Northern Ireland for a year, Martin and Janet came and stayed with me in Derry, and we had a memorable day in Belfast talking about nonviolence and the peace process with Gerry Adams. I remember speaking with him at the United Nations on peace; hearing him speak to church workers in Gallup, New Mexico, one of the poorest dioceses in the country; and having dinner with him and Bill Clinton at the Governor's Mansion in Santa Fe. He supported me at my first Mass in Washington, DC; my work with Pax Christi, the national Catholic peace movement; and my parish work in New Mexico. He's been such a strong support for me in all my work for the church, and for peace and justice, that I wonder if I could have done any of it without him. But I'm just one of many people that he has helped and befriended along the way. Martin is full of life and hope and love for others, and is incredibly generous. He amazes all of us.

In 1987 Martin was arrested at the Nevada Nuclear Test Site (now the Nevada National Security Site), along with six members of congress, fellow actors Kris Kristofferson and Robert Blake, and the noted scientist, Carl Sagan.[5] The site is located about sixty-five miles northwest of Las Vegas. The previous year Martin was arrested there with his friend, actor Matt Clark, as well as Sean Penn and his mother Eileen.[6] At that time Charles Champlin of the *Los Angeles Times* asked Martin what it was like to be arrested. Martin replied, "I always quote what Father Dan Berrigan told Mike Wallace during an interview. Being arrested is like a spiritual enema."[7] Fellow arrestee Rev. William "Bill" O'Donnell, a parish priest from Oakland, California, and a committed activist who was arrested hundreds of times over the years, celebrated Mass outside the gate during the demonstration.

Father John Dear recalls that beginning in 1989 Martin would drive with a group of friends, including Bill O'Donnell, Dan Berrigan, SJ, or Dr. Davida Coady and Louis Vitale, OFM, from San Francisco to the Nevada test site:

> It was crazy because it was such a long drive (and Martin would sometimes fly back to LA after). But we would set out and Martin would immediately start talking about Jesus. He would ask Bill, "When did Jesus know he was God?" And Martin would go on speculating. One time Bill answered, "When did you know you were a mystery?" Martin loved that question. Our conversation was always theological, always about God in very real ways. Martin has such a big heart and he really feels for people who suffer. He also has great hope, and great trust.

John Dear had just moved to Berkley in 1989 to study theology when news broke about the murders of six Jesuits and their housekeeper and her daughter in El Salvador. "I had known them," he recalls, "when I lived in El Salvador. We immediately organized a massive demonstration in the Bay area to protest the murders. When I told Martin about it he began talking with friends in Los Angeles and the next thing you know, they planned a demonstration in front of the downtown Los Angeles federal building."[8]

In February 2013, Martin and John Dear traveled together to a conference in Oslo, Norway, the International Campaign to Abolish Nuclear Weapons (ICAN), which took place before a gathering of 130 nations hosted by the Norwegian government on the abolition of nuclear arms. John wrote of their experience in the *National Catholic Reporter*:

> Martin began by thanking ICAN for their work to build a global abolition movement and encouraged everyone to keep at it. He read aloud their general call:
>
> > We call on states, international organizations, civil society organizations and everyone to acknowledge:
> >
> > - that any use of nuclear weapons would cause catastrophic humanitarian and environmental harm;
> > - that there is a universal humanitarian imperative to ban nuclear weapons, even for states that do not possess them;
> > - that the nuclear-armed states have an obligation to eliminate their nuclear weapons completely;
> > - and that we need to take immediate action to support a multilateral process of negotiations for a treaty banning nuclear weapons.
>
> During the evening event, we were interviewed together on stage about our work for peace over the last three decades: how we got involved, what we've done, where we get our energy, and what our hopes for peace are. Martin spoke about being in India during the making of the movie

Gandhi and how that experience led to an awakening of his faith and meeting Dan and Phil Berrigan, who pushed him to work publicly for peace. "Do you know why the movie *Gandhi* was such a success in Hollywood?" he asked the crowd. "Because *Gandhi* is what everyone in Hollywood wants to be—thin, tan and moral." The audience roared with laughter.

Martin's presence was a big boost to the many longtime activists, scholars, organizers and policymakers who attended the conference from around the world. Because of the non-stop media work he did, Martin has been seen and heard everywhere, probably by every Norwegian, encouraging Norway to lead the world toward the abolition of nuclear weapons.

In his opening speech, Martin quoted from Robert Kennedy's famous 1966 visit to South Africa: "Each time a man stands up for an ideal, or acts to improve the lot of others, or strikes out against injustice, he sends forth a tiny ripple of hope, and crossing each other from a million different centers of energy and daring, those ripples build a current that can sweep down the mightiest walls of oppression and resistance."

About that week in Oslo John concluded, "Martin and I felt those ripples of hope coming from around the world."[9]

One of the things Dear remembers most is Martin saying frequently that "Mother Teresa brought me back to the church but Dan Berrigan helps me to stay."

The Catholic Worker Movement

Following the murder of the Jesuit priests and their housekeeper and her daughter in El Salvador on November 16, 1989, the Los Angeles protest to cut US military aid to El Salvador joined ongoing Wednesday morning protests that were originally organized by the Office of the Americas. They continued for months. The protest was called the "Wednesday Coalition for Justice and Peace in Central America." The Catholic Workers of Los Angeles, including activist and author Jeff Dietrich and his wife Catherine Morris, were an integral part of these Wednesday morning acts of civil disobedience. Each Wednesday hundreds of nonviolent protesters marched from La Placita Church to the federal building and then a hundred or so of them blocked the entrance and were arrested. "They do this in protest of US policies toward El Salvador," reported *The Los Angeles Times,* "in memory of those killed in the war, protesters staged a symbolic 'die-in'; scores of masked demonstrators dropped to the sidewalk along Los Angeles Street below a full-sized skeleton crucified on an M16. 'Made in USA,' said the sign on the cross."

LA Times reporter Patt Morrison wrote the piece and she seems to make fun of those marching after the massacre of the Jesuits, saying that 234 "extremely polite" protesters were arrested at the January 17, 1990, event, including singer Jackson Browne and actors Ed Asner and Martin. "Martin Sheen, now with more than twenty arrests, for a time Wednesday was being so nice and letting everyone into the barricaded building that organizers saw the point of the blockade evaporating. So they moved another rank of demonstrators in front of him."[10] However overly civil the march may have appeared, it's a characteristic of what Martin brings to social activism.

At the Catholic Worker House, Jeff Dietrich and Catherine Morris, a former nun and also a Catholic Worker, talked with me about Martin's participation in the Wednesday Coalition marches and the weekly arrests for crossing the line. Martin would come to the house for coffee after, and because the Catholic Workers had to leave to prepare lunch at the kitchen located some distance away, it was someone's appointed task to stay and chat with him. "Catholic Workers are not so used to having guests for coffee on the mornings they cook for the homeless," Catherine told me with a smile.

For years now the Catholic Workers in Los Angeles have sponsored the Way of the Cross at 3:00 p.m. on Good Friday, and Martin participates every year. For the last twenty years they have begun the procession at the federal building downtown and then marched "to the darkest parts of the city," says Dietrich, "the federal court, the federal prison, the police department." Catherine Morris said that they don't have a permit to stop traffic, "So Martin steps up to halt traffic and no one gets upset."

"I don't think Martin ever met Dorothy Day, even when he was in New York, but it's her kind of Catholicism that is essential to the way he lives his faith," said Dietrich.

Catherine recalls that the BBC wanted to interview Martin a few years back and asked him to come into a studio for taping. But Martin said he would rather tape it at the Catholic Worker's Hospitality Kitchen, or as it is known among the homeless, "The Hippie Kitchen," on East 6th Street on Skid Row—and that the Catholic Workers should get the location fee. The BBC agreed.

Martin is one of the main supporters and contributors to the Catholic Workers Kitchen in Los Angeles. Dietrich believes that Martin "has a deep sense of a loving God who is on the side of the poor." Catherine describes Martin as "a really, really nice person. He will pose for pictures with anyone. When his son Emilio was shooting a film near the kitchen, Martin would come around to the garden. One day a guest told him he didn't understand how the filmmakers shot a certain scene in one of his movies and Martin took great pains to describe the process. Martin is just so kind and at ease with everyone."

Elizabeth McAlister

The influence of Dan Berrigan and Phil Berrigan on Martin as a Catholic activist for human rights, justice, and peace cannot be overstated. Elizabeth McAlister, Phil Berrigan's widow, also participated in social justice activities with Martin. She is a former religious of the Sacred Heart, member of Plowshares, and cofounder of Jonah House. Jonah House in Baltimore, Maryland, is a project dedicated to the support of "reluctant prophets" and human rights activists, that is, a network of individuals and communities who live by the interdependent pillars of nonviolence, resistance, and community. Elizabeth tells of Martin's friendship, support, and participation in their work. Her story about Martin fills out the story of Catholics who were and are willing to risk even jail time by speaking truth to power:

Martin was often in DC and, when free, would engage in social justice activities with a mutual friend, Mitch Snyder (1943–90), an ex-prisoner and staunch activist on behalf of the homeless. Mitch had been in prison at Danbury with Dan Berrigan and Phil Berrigan during the Vietnam era, converted to Catholicism, and learned resistance and service and a better, deeper way to live. Martin slept on the street with Mitch and the homeless and took his place on the line distributing meals and other necessities to the homeless. We often connected with him there.

In one of the actions that Jonah House facilitated with Mitch and the Community for Creative Non-Violence (CCNV), of which Mitch had become director, Phil and Martin marched together and together were sent to the DC jail. Phil reported that it was the strangest and loveliest of his many jail/prison experiences. The guards and inmates were all seeking words with Martin and asking for his autograph. It took so long that they were no sooner through the admission process when they had to begin the release process. "He humanized the whole scene," Phil said of Martin. It was a joyous experience. Would that they all were such.

In 1983 I was part of the Griffiss Plowshares action in which seven of us disarmed a B-52 and engines used for refueling planes at Griffiss Air Force Base in Rome, New York. We were arrested and tried in federal court in Syracuse, New York. A couple of times Martin could be seen sitting in the back row—as unobtrusively as he could—observing and supporting.

Prior to sentencing, there was a "Festival of Hope" in Syracuse on one night and another the next night in New York City. They were fundraiser celebrations for the Plowshares and local peace groups. Martin was present in Syracuse and spoke briefly in affirmation of our witness, and I also gave a short talk (the order of the day for such events is always short). Then he traveled with my family and me to New York for the festival there the next evening. Dan was ailing and not able to be present. We all wanted to see him, so we went to his apartment to find him flat on his back on the floor, such was his pain. Dan greeted us but quickly shooed us downtown to help get the NYC fundraiser celebrations moving. Martin spoke glowingly about this form of peace witness, underscoring the need for people to stand up, to take a stand.

A few days before McAllister and her companions were sentenced, CBS asked her to come to New York to appear on a news show. Martin appeared from the Los Angeles studio at the same time, offering support for their witness and wishing them well. All the Griffiss Plowshares were sentenced to terms in federal prison, and McAlister was given three years.

Martin gave us more than support. He gave his name, his presence. His words of support were palpable. I am certain he also lent financial support but that was not something I was tracking.

When in the area, it would sometimes happen that Martin would visit our community home in Baltimore. Sometimes it would be only a brief stopover en route to DC, sometimes with advance notice, sometimes not. Advance notice might allow for a supper party; no notice might mean that he'd go to the public school where our kids were and walk them home; our son Jerry's first grade teacher reminded me of that just recently.

Martin supported our move from the row house in Reservoir Hill, Baltimore, to St. Peter's Cemetery where we built a community house and have lived and worked since 1996. I know Martin contributed to that building fund. He walked into the house the morning of Phil's funeral (2002), paid his respects, and then was a participant in the procession from the house to the church through the streets of Baltimore. Amy Goodman, the amazing newswoman who founded and shapes the program *Democracy Now*, walked with Martin, interviewing him all the way. He sat with Phil's family through the funeral.

The last time Elizabeth McAlister recalls being with Martin was in January 2011. He and Emilio were presenting their film *The Way* to a large group of about five thousand students and many priests and nuns who were preparing for the annual March for Life. Before the film screening, Martin invited Elizabeth to the stage to talk about the justice mission of Jonah House. She concludes:

I do consider Martin a friend. He and his wife, Janet, came to Syracuse after I was released from prison and were part of the evening of celebration there. It was lovely and gracious of them to come. And he had come with his daughter Renée to visit me in prison and had a visit with one of my codefendants, as well. I recall an amazing exchange with them and, in spite of the fact that it was not a visiting day or normal visiting hours, he was made most welcome by all the prison staff who would find any reason to come near. He remains close to Dan Berrigan, and I trust that they will enjoy one another's company again before Dan departs from us. (He is now ninety-three and very frail).

I think Martin is motivated by love. He knew it close up with his family—especially with the Spanish part of his family—taking his own children to Spain so they could experience it. And though I do not see him often and am not in touch with him with any regularity, I know he is there and would be here for me if he humanly could and there were an emergency or need.

Mitch Snyder

Martin met Mitch Snyder when he was cast to play Mitch in *Samaritan: The Mitch Snyder Story*. It aired on television in May 1986. Mitch had joined the CCNV in 1972 and became its director. (A Paulist priest, Fr. Ed Guinan, founded the CCNV to oppose the Vietnam War and educate people about nonviolence; the center soon opened a soup kitchen as well to meet the growing needs of people.) In the 1980s Mitch became concerned about the increasingly desperate situation of the homeless. Countless veterans living on the streets of Washington, DC, and the deinstitutionalization of thousands of mentally ill people raised the homeless population dramatically, both in Washington, DC, and nationally.[11] The film traces Mitch's efforts to force President Reagan to give the CCNV a building to provide shelter and sanctuary to the homeless. He went on a hunger strike that nearly killed him. It worked. President Reagan signed an order on November 4, 1984, giving the CCNV the Federal City Shelter—then the largest of its kind in America.

Although it's a low budget made-for-television movie, *Samaritan* maintains its relevance today because homelessness in America continues to increase as the gap between rich and poor widens. Martin's passion for the homeless in the film is convincing, probably because Mitch tutored a willing student who was becoming more aware of deep social ills in the world. Cicely Tyson's performance as Muriel, a homeless woman originally from Jamaica who teaches Mitch and his companions how to survive on the streets by keeping warm above steam vents, earned an Image Award.

Later, Mitch and Martin were arrested one night for trying to prevent the police from closing a subway entrance where the homeless were taking shelter. While in jail overnight, Martin and Mitch came up with the idea of the Grate American Celebrity Sleep Out. Though only a few entertainment celebrities participated, namely Dennis Quaid, Brian Dennehy, and Grant Cramer, more than one hundred persons showed up on March 3 in thirty-degree weather to draw support for a $500 million emergency aid bill to aid the homeless. It passed two days later. Two members of Congress were there to huddle over steam vents with them: Mickey Leland (1944–89), who worked to promote social justice and find solutions to hunger at home and around the world, and John Conyers, one of the founders of the Congressional Black Caucus. Snyder told the *New York Times* that even if they did not get the money "this [effort] is to guarantee that people across this country will wake up tomorrow thinking a little more about the homeless."[12]

In 1988 Martin narrated an award-winning PBS documentary on Mitch, *Promises to Keep*. Some feel this film better represented the real Mitch who, in reality, was more intense than depicted in *Samaritan*. His demons got the best of him, however, and sadly Mitch Snyder took his own life at the shelter on July 5, 1990.

Crossing the Line

For nonviolent peace and human rights activists to "cross the line" means that they are willing to engage in civil disobedience and be arrested for their peaceful actions. Martin used to keep track of how many times he was arrested by his age but after sixty-six times (some say sixty-seven), he gave up. And there's also the matter of his serving a three-year probation sentence for crossing the line at a protest at the Vandenberg Air Base in California in 2000 that would lead him to modify the degree of his participation in protests.

Carmen, Martin's sister, says that she is very proud of her brother's activism and that she wishes she could be as brave as he is. She has only accompanied him on one protest. It was in Nevada for the anniversary of the atomic bombings of Hiroshima and Nagasaki, sponsored by the Office of the Americas (OOA). Her description of being with Martin for the march and crossing the line is very personal:

> When I arrived in Malibu for my annual family visit, Martin told me that he had made a reservation for me to come with him and some other activists to Las Vegas, but that if I did not want to go, that was okay. I knew they would be trespassing on military property and they would probably be arrested, and I was afraid to do that. Martin said I was not to worry because a lot of people did not cross the line, and they were the ones to get the others out of jail the next day. He assured me that I would be meeting very good people and that they would take care of me. I decided to go.

We went with Fr. John Dear; Fr. Louis Vitale, OFM; and Dr. Davida Coady and her husband, Tom Gorham. I felt like I was in a car full of saints, especially with Fr. Louis, who was fasting and would not even suck on a piece of candy. Once we got to the meeting place to begin the march, Martin was very busy with a lot of people who wanted to talk with him. And like he said, I did meet a group of very friendly ladies and they took care of me. I got attached to one particular lady, Mary, very soon. She was about my age, a teacher like myself and with a similar background.

I asked Mary if she was going to cross the line and she said no, she wasn't going to cross this time. I told her I was glad to hear that, and we promised to stick together. When it was almost dark somebody came over to me and asked me how I was and that my brother was concerned about me. I told him I was fine and to tell my brother not to worry about me. I was in good hands.

Soon after that we began the march, and it was then very dark but most of us were carrying flashlights. It was very moving, and I was happy to be there and to be a part of this demonstration. As we began to walk down to the military complex, everybody began singing the hymn "Amazing Grace," and it was so powerful. I couldn't believe how strong I felt. Mary and I were walking arm in arm. We were very close to the line and suddenly I knew I would be crossing over. Just then Mary asked me, "Carmen, are you going to cross?" I said, "Yes." And she said, "I am glad to hear that because I am coming with you!" So we walked down, joined at the hip like frightened school children, listening to the government warning that we were trespassing as we crossed. We didn't stop and headed for the pen set up for women. We never looked back. When we got inside we turned around and saw a huge crowd of women coming down the hill behind us. They were all singing and smiling. It was so uplifting.

I had no idea where my brother was, but I assumed he was in the pen for the men because he had been at the head of the march. Inside the women's pen there was a lot of laughing and singing. I was having a great time, and I forgot all about what might happen. After a long time I heard my name being called out over the loud speaker and I went up to the gate. The policeman told me that my brother had told him that I had to get on a flight that night; I didn't but I said I did. I started out the gate, but like in the movies he put out his arm and said, "Not so fast lady! You have to talk to that policeman over there when he calls you."

A short while later that policeman, a big guy, as big as an armoire, called me over for questioning. I was really scared. I hugged Mary and the other ladies and said goodbye. The big policeman turned out to be a very civil and charming man. He took down all my information and told me that he didn't think the law would be getting in touch with me but if they did, I was not to ignore the summons if it came. We shook hands, and I waved to Mary and my new friends. I made my way back up to the main gate and there I found Fr. John Dear waiting for me. He took me back up to where we had left the car and there was my brother and the other activists we came with. Martin said that when I told the messenger to tell him that he was not to worry, and that I was in good hands, he knew I was going to cross the line. I hadn't known it myself, but he was right. I am very glad that I had this experience with my brother, and now I understand what he is up against. This time was not really as dangerous as others are when there is no media coverage to keep the police in line. I know Martin has been treated like a criminal when he has been speaking out for peace and social justice and that no matter what, he will continue to do so. I am so proud to be his sister.

Cesar Chavez

Martin met Cesar Chavez in 1988 when Chavez was in the midst of an epic thirty-six-day fast. The purpose of his fast was to draw attention to the use of pesticides on table grapes and the cancer clusters that were affecting farm workers and their families, especially children in California's Central Valley and beyond. It was the beginning of a friendship that would last until Cesar's death in 1993 and continue with the family. Paul Chavez, Cesar's son and now president of the Cesar Chavez Foundation, said,

> It was Martin's relationship with Fr. Bill O'Donnell that brought Martin to meet my father during his last fast at La Paz (Keene, California). Martin came five or six times, I think, and was there when my father broke his fast on August 21, 1988. I recall at the end of the fast, after the Mass, my father could hardly walk, but he made it a point to go and thank people, and one of them was Martin. They didn't spend a lot of time together after that, but their kinship was very strong.

Arturo Rodriguez, president of the United Farm Workers of America (UFW), recalls that when Cesar Chavez began his last fast:

> We invited celebrities to come and join in solidarity and to speak out in support of the farm workers. Martin came several times, and I got to spend time with him, even though I was busy coordinating everything going on around the fast. Knowing who he was, his status, that he took the time, I came to respect him a lot.
>
> When Cesar passed away so suddenly in 1993, we did not expect it, and Martin came to visit us. He continues to be involved and engaged in our work and is often part of

demonstrations and events. He came to the UFW convention fund-raising dinner in 2012; he makes public service announcements for different campaigns and supports immigrant families. He's very interested in immigration reform and supporting the immigrant farm workers in our country.

Martin's involvement with the UFW continues to this day.

In a scene that did not make it into the 2014 award-winning documentary *Cesar's Last Fast* by Richard R. Perez, Martin describes his first meeting with Cesar Chavez, arranged by Fr. Bill O'Donnell. The priest was one of Cesar's closest friends. Bill went in Cesar's room first to see if he would receive Martin and his wife, Janet. Cesar agreed to do so. At that time Martin was a heavy smoker, and he was very nervous about meeting the great man. Janet told him to put out his cigarette, but he told her to go on in ahead of him while he finished smoking. When Martin entered the room he was deeply impressed with how small and frail Cesar was. He watched as Janet kissed Cesar's hand and he, in turn, kissed hers. When Martin kneeled down, he kissed Cesar's hand and when Cesar kissed his, he was greatly embarrassed because "it must have been like kissing an ash tray." At that moment Martin decided to fast from smoking and that lasted several years.[13] He started smoking again when he was doing *The West Wing* (1999–2006) but finally quit in 2007 and has not smoked since. One of the reasons Cesar decided to end the fast was because people like Martin and Jessie Jackson promised to keep the fast going, three days at a time.

Today Paul Chavez says that there is a photo of his grandmother, Juana Chavez, and Martin on the bookshelf in Cesar's office as well as a straw cowboy hat, the kind that farm workers wear, that Martin autographed for his father years ago, using his real name: "To Cesar from Ramon."

Mayor of Malibu

In 1989 the Malibu, California, chamber of commerce named Martin Honorary Mayor of Malibu for the year. Martin took his role seriously, however, and his consistent commitment to justice and peace made news around the country when he declared Malibu a "nuclear-free zone, a sanctuary for aliens and the homeless and a protected environment for all life, wild and tame."[14] The chamber of commerce was somewhat taken aback by Martin's proactive approach to an honorary position and briefly considered rescinding their decision, but in the end, Martin completed his term.

Martin's brother Conrad died in Dayton in November of 1989. Conrad had been a teacher in Dayton and spent some years teaching in Alabama, as well.

School of the Americas Watch

For many years Martin has been advocating for the close of the School of the Americas, a military training base in Columbus, Georgia. Roy Bourgeois, at that time a Maryknoll priest,[15] founded the School of the Americas Watch (SOAW) in 1990 as a campaign to close the post. Bourgeois called the institution the "School of Assassins" ". . . for the people of Latin America who have been the victims of US foreign policy and this school . . . because you do not teach democracy through the barrel of a gun."[16]

The U.S. Army School of the Americas at Fort Benning was founded in 1946 to train Latin American military personnel in anti-communist, counterinsurgency tactics. Personnel trained at the SOA have long been accused of gross human rights violations, including the assassination of Archbishop Oscar Romero in 1980. In January 2001 the name of the school was changed to the Western Hemisphere

Institute for Security Cooperation (WHINSEC).[17] While the name changed, nothing else did, according to John Dear. "The SOA/WHINSEC continues to train Latin American militaries and death squads."

The SOA Watch demonstrations are held each year to coincide with the anniversary of the killing of six Jesuits and their housekeeper and her daughter on November 16, 1989. They were killed at the José Simeón Cañas Central American University (UCA) in San Salvador. The victims were Fathers Ignacio Ellacuría, rector of the University; Ignacio Martín-Baró, vice-rector; Segundo Montes, director of the Human Rights Institute; Amando López, Joaquín López y López, and Juan Ramón Moreno, all teachers at UCA; and Julia Elba Ramos and her daughter, Celina Mariceth Ramos."[18] Nineteen of the twenty-six killers were SOA graduates, according to CNN.[19] It is known that the Salvadoran army's Atlacatl Battalion, created in 1980 by the School of the Americas, carried out the attack, as reported in the "United Nations Truth Commission on El Salvador" report in 1993.[20]

Martin writes about meeting Bourgeois for the first time:

> As a result of these [SOA Watch] efforts, Father Roy became the obvious choice for the 1996 Office of the Americas Peace and Justice Award. But as he was unable to attend the ceremony in Los Angeles, fellow board member and prominent filmmaker, Haskell Wexler, and I were asked to present it to him in prison where he was doing time for crossing the line at an SOA protest.
>
> We arrived in Atlanta on a sweltering afternoon at the height of the Summer Olympics and went straight to the prison for a pre-arranged meeting. The city was on edge, following a bombing in the Olympic Park, which had killed one person and injured dozens of others a few days earlier.

But the atmosphere in the prison was surprisingly relaxed. In fact, beyond the routine security, we were hardly noticed at all. A lone guard escorted us to a near-empty cafeteria where we were greeted by Roy, a disarmingly youthful-looking man with a distinctive Southern accent that revealed, as I soon discovered, his Louisiana Cajun roots. After presenting him with the award, we sat down for a lengthy interview on his life and work, which Haskell filmed for showing at the annual OOA [Office of the Americas] fundraiser in Los Angeles the following November. Thus began a warm and rewarding friendship that led me on several occasions to join him and thousands of others in the annual nonviolent peaceful demonstrations against the SOA, culminating [for many] in trespass and arrest at Fort Benning.[21]

But Roy remembers that visit differently. In a way, his version reflects on Martin's generous character:

Martin and his friend (Haskell Wexler) made a special trip from Los Angeles on behalf of the OOA, a peace organization, to visit me and bring me this little award. The guards were giving me a hard time in prison. The guards, for whatever reason, didn't like protesters. But when Martin arrived, people really flocked to him—the guards and the inmates who saw him from a distance were excited. The guards wanted his autograph, which he gave them. After that visit, the guards, who had been giving me a hard time, changed. They became very respectful and kind to me. I remember writing to Martin to thank him, that his visit to me in prison made it so much better.

Bourgeois described Martin's participation in the SOA Watch protests in that same interview. His lengthy remarks create a record of the involvement of people who are motivated by faith, indeed leading, protests for social justice:

Martin came to the vigil on a number of occasions, and this is how I first got to know him. We would ask Martin to speak from the stage set up outside the gates of Fort Benning, Georgia. Some fifteen to twenty thousand people would come to the gates. Martin was so warm and outgoing. When he spoke it was from the heart and people loved him.

What I liked about him especially is how he was so warm and hospitable to young people. His sincerity and goodness put them at ease. They wanted to shake his hand and get autographs, which he did so gladly. He really connected to young people with sincerity and goodness. So many wanted to talk to him. He made them feel like he was a friend and inspired them to take home the love, peace, and non-violence they had experienced at the protest.

A couple of times he didn't want to stay in the Marriott, but asked to stay in a modest hotel. He also asked if we could find him a church where he could go to Mass. So he stayed at the Howard Johnson's and he'd go to Holy Family Catholic Church. It was very important to him.

I remember one of the vigils during the years when Martin played the president on *The West Wing*. There were about seventeen thousand people at the protest. We were right in front of the main gate of Fort Benning and the crowd reached way down the street. The SOA was right down the road inside the gate. I will never forget Martin's closing remarks on the stage: "As your acting president, commander-in-chief, I hereby order that the SOA," and he turned and pointed to it, "be closed forever!" People went wild! They started howling and clapping and laughing. It was a very joyful moment. His words ignited the crowd, and it was so funny.

He is open to critics, too. I remember in the early days, maybe his first trip here, his message was very religious. He ended his talk by inviting the crowd to pray the Our Father. There were some very polite college students who came to me after and asked, "Could you tell Martin that we are not all Catholic here?" They were upset, or perhaps the better word is offended, because people were there from all faith traditions, Jews, Buddhists, too. So I said, "Why don't you tell him yourselves?"

When Martin came off the stage, I told him there were a couple of college students who wanted to chat with him. Martin listened to them and thanked them for their criticism. Rather than getting upset, as some would, or cutting them short, Martin listened and thanked them and said he would try to be more sensitive in the future and he was. Then he hugged them. They left feeling happy and joyful. That was Martin. He embraced and accepted their criticism in a gentle kind way. From then on he used more inclusive language in his remarks.

Martin has visited Latin America numerous times for humanitarian reasons, including trips to Guatemala and El Salvador with Fr. John Dear and to Nicaragua with the Office of the Americas (OOA). Martin went with family members visiting from Spain to Tijuana, Mexico, with the Mexico Mission outreach program run by his parish church, Our Lady of Malibu, in January 2014, to deliver goods to La Morita Mission. In 2013 he and costar Rooney Mara went to Rio de Janeiro, Brazil (it happened to occur during World Youth Day) to visit a huge garbage dump to prepare for his role as a Catholic missionary priest in director Stephen Daldry's 2014 film *Trash*. The film is an adaptation of the 2011 children's novel by Andy Mulligan about three boys in a poor, developing country who grow up on a dump. The boys' discovery of a leather bag in the dump unleashes powerful forces that will do anything to get it back.

In the 2007 documentary *On the Line*, Martin tells the protesters:

What we do, what all of us try to do by our lives, if we're inspired by the Gospel, is to find some measure to unite the will of the spirit to the work of the flesh," Martin says. "We don't really have a sense of what our action is doing in the Third World, so we have to have our consciousness enlarged, so we see ourselves as part of a universal community and not limited to the United States. . . . I find that people who go to the Third World, whether for pleasure or work or for social justice, are changed. The sights and sounds, the smells of the Third World are indelible. You never forget those and they draw you further into the heart of Third World communities."[22]

When asked what it was like to cross the line at Fort Benning in 2006, Martin replied, "It's a very profound experience. I've had the honor of being arrested here several times and the last time was with my good friend, Fr. Bill O'Donnell."

The Office of the Americas

Blase Bonpane and Theresa Bonpane are the founders of the Office of the Americas (OOA), a nonprofit international peace and justice educational organization. They met Martin through John Chapman, who had been a production assistant on *Apocalypse Now*. He asked the couple to consult on a film about Central America and brought along Martin for the meeting. "That was the beginning of a long friendship with Martin," says Blase. "He was quickly responsive to just about every gathering or demonstration we had for peace in Central America." Today, Martin serves on the board of the organization.

In 1983 the OOA had outgrown the couple's home and Rev. Carlyle Gill, the rector of St. Augustine by-the-Sea Episcopal Church in Santa Monica, California, very generously provided office space for the organization. A few days later Martin called to say he had been given $25,000 for his role as a priest in the 1982 made-for-television film *Choices of the Heart*, the story of Jean Donovan. Donovan was a young laywoman, played by Melissa Gilbert, who along with three women religious, Maura Clarke, MM, Ita Ford, MM, and Dorothy Kazel, OSU, was beaten, raped, and murdered by a Salvadoran military death squad (believed to be trained at the SOA) on December 2, 1980. Martin wanted some suggestions for distributing his earnings to five solidarity groups. When Theresa told Martin of their new office, he donated $5,000 for the OOA. "Since that day, Martin has been an active member of our executive board as well as a warm and personal friend of our family."

Blase tells of one trip he and Martin took together to Nicaragua and an encounter at a major US university:

> Martin agreed to come with me to Nicaragua during the peak of the US-sponsored Contra War, where weapons illegally purchased from Iran were used to kill forty thousand innocent Nicaraguans. After being in the war zones all day, we were returning to Managua at night when a raft of shooting took place just in front of our bus. Martin showed a great deal of courage in the wake of this gunfire. We all were relieved to understand finally that the shooting came from Sandinista troops, as a signal to stay back from their defensive position until all was clear.
>
> Martin was also calm under fire in the United States. We traveled together to Tulane University in Louisiana to speak to a large gathering of students regarding the illegal US war in Nicaragua. In the back of the crowd a half-drunk group of attendees were waving a US flag. One of the hecklers shouted: "We want our money back!" Martin

came down from the stage and said, "I have your money right here, but there is one condition, you must come up and shake my hand." The student complied and the audience clapped vigorously.

Martin is at home on this planet. He is a living voice of compassion. We asked for his participation so very many times and he responded graciously. Martin is always as available, whether to janitors and bus boys or his fellow celebrities.

And then there were the times we were arrested. I am sure the count of his arrests for civil disobedience is at least sixty. In 1990, after the killings of the Salvadoran Jesuits, we would all meet on Wednesday mornings at 7:00 a.m. at the Mother Church of Los Angeles, La Nuestra Senora Reina de Los Angeles (also known as La Placita). We would pray with the pastor, Fr. Luis Olivares, and then march to the federal building to protest the Central American wars. The group frequently included celebrities such as Kris Kristofferson, Jackson Browne, Edward Asner, Haskell Wexler, and David Clennon. We always insisted that those who intended to be arrested that day would segregate themselves from those who did not choose to be arrested. We did not want anyone to be surprised by an arrest they did not expect.

One of those days, I had not intended to be arrested, but Martin came along with some vials of blood to throw on the marble identification sign: United States Federal Building. I could not resist. I poured the blood with him. For me, that was a surprise arrest, and even though I kept thinking of all the work I had to do at the office, I went ahead.

After some time in the cells, we were brought before an ancient judge. In contrast, the prosecutors looked like teenagers. The prosecutors testified that we had damaged federal property. The judge asked them about the nature of the damage. The prosecutors said that it was blood, and that it had been washed off the marble sign. The judge said, "That was not property damage, that was littering." So we walked away free that day. I must mention that after 9/11, such infractions have been met with as much as six months in prison.

Martin expresses his worldview very clearly: "I am a human being first and an actor second!" That is the great quality we have always seen in him in his daily life as well as on that hot day in Managua when he insisted on donating his blood at a clinic for the Nicaraguan wounded.

Mother Teresa

Martin always attributes the inspiration for his return to the church to Mother Teresa. Martin had read much about Mother Teresa and admired her greatly. In addition to almost meeting her during the filming of *Gandhi*, he met her three times in the early 1990s.

Joe Cosgrove, Martin's attorney, nonviolent peace-protester colleague, good friend, and Notre Dame graduate in law and theology, invited Martin to go to Rome to meet Mother Teresa in April 1991 on a peace mission. Little did Martin know that it was only he and Joe on that peace mission! Cosgrove was determined to ask Mother Teresa to take a letter to Pope John Paul II, whom she was scheduled to meet the next day, asking him to allow Cosgrove, as a lawyer, to represent the Vatican at The Hague to propose a way to end the Gulf War. The Vatican had been the only "country" to unilaterally object to the Gulf War, and only nations, not individuals or groups, could appeal to The Hague. Mother Teresa met with them, heard them out, and agreed to speak to the Holy Father. She then invited Joe and Martin to Mass at 5:00 a.m. the next day—and the war ended that morning. Joe told Martin, "Don't mess with Mother."[23]

In late 1991 and early 1992 Martin was in New York, performing at Tony Randall's National Actors Theater production of Arthur Miller's *The Crucible*. During that time Martin and Janet met Mother Teresa at a Bronx church where she received the final vows of two of her sisters.

In 1992 Martin went to Tijuana, Mexico, to meet Mother Teresa where she was recovering at the Missionaries of Charity convent after heart surgery. John Dear, Martin's good friend, recounts:

> There had been a call for help, and Martin helped raise money to purchase a vehicle for Mother Teresa's sisters, the Missionaries of Charity, to bring health services to poor people in Tijuana. Tony Robbins, the motivational speaker, asked Martin if he would accompany him to bring the vehicle to Tijuana and meet Mother Teresa. Mother was only four feet ten and Tony is a towering six feet eight. He asked Mother, "How did you get to be the most famous person in the world? And she looked up to him and said, "Jesus." Robbins continued, "No, I mean, you have two thousand nuns in a hundred countries. How did you do that?" Mother responded, "Jesus." "No," Robbins continued, "You've raised millions of dollars for the poor and helped so many people. How do you do it?" "Jesus," she answered again. "No," Robbins insisted. "How is it that you have been in every newspaper and magazine in the entire planet and are so greatly admired?" "Jesus," she answered again with a smile. Martin loved that exchange.

Helena Buscema, a singer and musician, has been a friend of Martin and his family for more than twenty-five years:

> He loves Mother Teresa and introduced me to her ways and outlook with this quote, "Never worry about numbers. Help one person at a time and always start with the person

nearest you." And so I have tried to live by her example. In 2005 I was going to Croatia, and Martin told me I should check out the Isle of Brac. In the early 2000s officials there wanted to commission a sculpture of his likeness because of his human rights work. Instead he suggested that they commission one of Mother Teresa and the officials agreed.

In 2002 Martin went to Croatia to film *Mercy of the Sea*, in which he and his daughter Renée Estevez both appeared. When filming concluded he was on hand for the unveiling of the sculpture created by a local artist Petar Jaksic. It is the first monument in the world to honor Mother Teresa.[24]

PREDA

In the early '90s Martin went to the Philippines where he accompanied Fr. Shay Cullen, an Irish priest of the Missionary Society of St. Columban, to visit people who lived in a massive garbage dump in Quezon City. Cullen had founded a nongovernmental agency called PREDA (People's Recovery, Empowerment and Development Foundation) in 1974 "to save children from abuse, prison and exploitation." "It was so horrible; the smell was so overwhelming," Martin said. "Disposable diapers were piled up and contaminating the environment; the smell, the brown color of the water, and the children walking in the muck up to their thighs—I was knocked off center by it all."

When Cyclone Yolanda (also known as Haiyan) struck in November 2013, Janet contacted Fr. Cullen to ask how they could help. The priest was on his way to the affected area and requested funds so they could get what they specifically needed, such as sacks of rice. The Sheens continue to raise funds for the work of PREDA and the recovery work after

Yolanda. Martin remains impressed by something Fr. Cullen once told him, "In all of these Third World places, when there are catastrophes and disasters, pedophiles come in and troll for children. There are hundreds of orphans, maybe thousands, and these people wear a Red Cross pin or a hat and the children follow them and are never seen again. Our work is to make sure children are placed with real agencies."

Seamless Garment Life Ethic

Martin is pro-life and adheres to the consistent ethic of life outlined in 1983 by Joseph Cardinal Bernardin.[25] This "seamless garment" approach means that as a Christian he supports care for the environment and opposes all forms of violence, including war, nuclear weapons, the death penalty, racism, sexism—and abortion. "I am totally opposed to any interference and ending of life, I believe in all of life."[26]

Martin works to end the death penalty with the California organization Death Penalty Focus, headed by fellow actor and activist Mike Farrell. This has not been their only journey together. As Martin writes in the foreword to the *M*A*S*H* star's memoir, *Just Call Me Mike*,[27] there is a cost to being who you say you are:

> There is more than a grain of truth in the old saying, "No good deed goes unpunished." The cost of reaching out to improve the lot of others can be very high indeed, depending on the depth of one's commitment and the effectiveness of one's efforts. The plain truth is that people who work for peace and justice or strive against corruption, ignorance, and apathy, for example, will pay dearly on every level of their public and private lives. Yet given a choice "to do or not to do," committed souls will not alter course; they cannot *not* "do" and still be themselves. I don't mean

to imply that activists anticipate failure—on the contrary. But "success" is measured in tiny increments, while the planting of seeds for the future is essential. For a dedicated person, one key form of success is the satisfaction of taking the right civil or moral stand, however unpopular, and suffering the consequences. . . .

I recently participated in another peace march and rally against the war in Iraq in downtown Los Angeles. Suddenly, I looked to my left and saw Mike hobbling the route on crutches (the result of a broken ankle from a motorcycle accident). The poignant image brought to mind the old Irish tale of a successful man who arrives at the gates of heaven and demands entry. "Of course," St. Peter says, just show us your scars." "I have no scars," the man replies. "What a pity," St. Peter says, "was there nothing worth fighting for?"

In 2012 Martin narrated an ad in favor of California's Proposition 34, "Death Penalty Initiative Statute" to end the death penalty:

"Freedom, it's such an essential part of our lives," he says in the ad. "It's hard to imagine it being taken away without just cause. But it can be, and it has been. Franky Carrillo was wrongly convicted of murder. It took twenty years to prove he was innocent." Then Franky Carrillo speaks: "With the death penalty, we always risk executing an innocent person. Let's replace it with life in prison without the possibility of parole, so we'd never make a fatal mistake." Martin concludes by saying, "Vote yes on 34. It's justice that works for everyone."[28]

Proposition 34 was narrowly defeated, but Martin and many others still believe that the death penalty is inherently wrong and inhuman, and continue their work to abolish it.

One of Martin's favorite episodes of *The West Wing* was season one's "Take This Sabbath Day." In this episode President Bartlet wrestles with the death penalty and an impending execution. He has prayed and no light has come, he tells his priest friend, Fr. Tom Cavanaugh (played by Karl Malden). Though the priest counsels him to pay greater attention to what God is saying, Bartlet makes the decision to let the execution go ahead. Rather than being pro-capital punishment, the episode shows how obstinate and deaf those in power can be to the truth that all of life is precious and that the state does not have the right to kill its own citizens.

These days Martin is currently working to free Jon-Adrian Velazquez, a New York man sentenced to twenty-five years to life in prison. The conviction is without evidence and based on what Velazquez's supporters say is misidentification.[29] Martin and his friend Joe Cosgrove are also working to halt the impending execution of Hubert Lester Michael, Jr., a convicted murderer, in Pennsylvania. In 2012, the U.S. Third Circuit Court of Appeals granted him a stay. The court lifted it on June 30, 2014. Pennsylvania Governor Tom Corbett signed a death warrant on July 24, 2014, for Michael to be executed in September of 2014 but another stay was issued before the scheduled execution on September 22. The last execution in Pennsylvania was in 1999. Corbett, a Catholic, has signed at least four death warrants in 2014. More than two hundred people are on Pennsylvania's death row.

Martin Sheen has been involved in environmental issues through Greenpeace and the Sea Shepherd Conservation Society for years. On October 18, 2014, Sea Shepherd named their newest research vessel after Martin: the *R/V Martin Sheen*.

The Path of Nonviolence

At a protest at the Los Alamos National Laboratories in New Mexico in 1999, marking the fifty-fourth anniversary of the United States dropping the atomic bomb on Nagasaki, Martin told journalist and host of *Democracy Now!* Amy Goodman, "I work for NBC to make a living. I do this to stay alive."[30] This formula would be tested in the years to come.

In October 2000 Martin was arrested for trespassing with several others at Vandenberg Air Force Base. Their intention was to deliver a message to the base commander about their opposition to the militarization of space.

In June 2001 Martin appeared in federal court in Los Angeles. Because of his commitment to his family and contractual obligations to NBC's *The West Wing*, at the suggestion of his attorney friend Joe Cosgrove, Martin chose to take a guilty plea. He was sentenced to a $500 fine and three-years probation. He thus avoided a trial and possible prison time. He would have to find a way to live out his faith in action and yet avoid crossing the line and trespassing or he would be sent to prison immediately.

In 2003 the invasion of Iraq became inevitable. Martin and Joe appealed to the court to waive his probation so he could cross the line, but it was turned down. Martin commented:

> So I would go to rallies and speak, but when we reached the line, I would back off. One of the big protests about the war was a wonderful event organized by women in March 2003. They strung up a clothesline across the front of the federal building in downtown Los Angeles and hung children's clothing from it to symbolize that children were dying in the war. I knew how precarious my situation was, so I put a piece of duct tape across my mouth and wrote "Peace" on it so I wouldn't speak. I had to remember that if I crossed the line and joined those women, I'd go to jail. I had to make a statement but I also had to avoid arrest to continue my work on *The West Wing*.

Martin had written a poem/prayer based on the prayer *Make Me an Instrument of Your Peace* (attributed to

St. Francis of Assisi) and the poem "Where the Mind is Without Fear" by the Nobel laureate Rabindranath Tagore. He wrote it in 2003 and read it as part of a speech at the protest against the US war on Iraq in front of the federal building in Los Angeles:

There Can Be No Victory
In order to prepare for war, you must not be sensitive or poetic or humorous, you must not be self effacing or reflective, sentimental or forgiving. You must not be tentative, compassionate or light-hearted.

On the contrary, in order to prepare for war, you must be clear, uncompromising and confident. You must look life square in the eye and choose death.
Lord, make us instruments of your peace.

This war was a foregone conclusion since September 20, 2002, when the United States declared a policy of "first strike option," including nuclear first strike, against any nation it perceived as a threat. In one year, we'd gone from protection to paranoia.

Lord, make us instruments of your peace.

Nationalism and patriotism have become the gods of our idolatry, and those opposed to the madness of this war are told to give thanks and praise for living in a country that tolerates such dissent, as if basic human rights and personal conscience were given by the gracious hand of any state.

Lord, make us instruments of your peace.

By some demented form of logic, the men, women and children of Iraq are relegated to collateral damage, as the dogs of war slouch toward Baghdad.

Lord, make us instruments of your peace.

We are left empty and trembling at the level of confidence placed in power and violence, and the level of arrogance it has inspired in our national leadership. And so Lord, we beg you, descend with us into the depths of our powerlessness and fear, and awaken there, Lord, the power of nonviolent transformation, where we may discover fire for the second time. And then, Lord, let the light from that fire make every thought, word, and deed a reflection of loving, nonviolent resistance to every wretched form of violence, so that we may be made worthy of the long-promised blessings reserved for the peacemakers and those who show mercy.

Lord, make us instruments of your peace.

Lord, we pray you make us instruments of your peace so we may lift up the world and all its people to a place where their heart is without fear, and their head is held high, where knowledge is free, where the world has not been broken up into fragments by narrow, domestic wars, where words come out from the depths of truth, where tireless striving stretches its arms towards perfection, where the clear stream of reason has not lost its way into the dreary desert sands of dead habit, where the mind is led forward by Thee into every thought and action into that heaven of freedom.

My Father, let my country awake!

Martin's commitment to social justice, peace, disarmament, and humanitarian causes, the environment, and nonviolent activism has cost him professionally. Activist and journalist David Kupfer spoke with Martin at the Archdiocese of Los Angeles Religious Education Congress in 2003 after Martin had spoken to a group of eight hundred catechists. Kupfer asked Martin, "What did you mean when you said, 'Your faith has to cost you something, otherwise you have to question its value'"? Martin responded: "Once you follow a path

of nonviolence and social justice, it won't take you long before you come into conflict with the culture, with society. You
can't know what is at stake or how much it is going to cost
you until you get in the game. That's the only way, and the
level of cost is equal to the level of involvement."[31]

In 2010 Martin was given the "Nuclear-Free Future Award"
by the Franz Moll Foundation for the Coming Generations:[32]
"For waging peace with his resolute convictions and inspiring
others to follow his enduring example." Since he could not
be present at the ceremony in New York City, he sent his
regrets and comments that reveal the principles by which he
lives:

> Militarism, nationalism and materialism have become the
> gods of our idolatry at the expense of our humanity, leav-
> ing us trembling at the level of confidence placed in the
> power of violent weapons, including nuclear weapons, and
> the level of arrogance that they have inspired in our na-
> tional and world leaders.
>
> We must take responsibility to put an end to the deadly
> nuclear cycle from the mining of uranium on indigenous
> lands, to the reckless disposal of the nuclear waste, to the
> destruction of generations of people and the environment
> from nuclear power plants and nuclear weapons. We must
> acknowledge that this legacy of radioactivity is an abom-
> ination toward all creation.
>
> Henceforth, let us resolve to make every thought, every
> word and every deed a reflection of nonviolent resistance
> to the very wretched form of nuclear violence as we strive
> for the courage to do justice, oppose evil and in the end be
> made worthy of the long promised blessing reserved for
> peacemakers and for those who sow mercy."[33]

CHAPTER FIVE

Spirituality of
an Activated Catholic

Martin's close friends will tell you that he loves to talk about theology, about God, Jesus, Mary, the Mass, the sacraments, the gospels, and humanity. Martin tells a story to describe his theology or understanding of God:

I was at St. Monica's Church in Santa Monica one Sunday before the most recent changes in the prayers of the Mass were made.[1] Msgr. Torgerson, one of the greatest preachers, had just finished his homily, and he began the recitation of the Creed. There was this guy behind me, who knew all the prayers of the Mass and was so loud and overbearing, well, I just sat in silence. When we got to the part of the Creed where it used to say, "He was born of the Virgin Mary and became man," this annoying man said with great passion instead, "and he was born of the Virgin Mary *and became human*!" I was so struck by that. It made me reflect on what it truly meant for God to become like one of us! Now every time I pray the Creed I say *human* because when you think of the difference between "man" and "human," well, it's remarkable. Jesus became one of us!

When I think of Jesus as human, I think of the mystery of God becoming human. Did you ever think of how long God may have been trying to send the Messiah, but because God would not force himself on anyone, because we have free will, it didn't work. And maybe the person God asked said, "No" or "Are you kidding? You want me to do what?" And then an angel goes to this little girl, Mary, and asks her, and she says "yes."

Father William "Bill" Kerze has known Martin since he first came to the parish as pastor in 1995. "I know Martin mostly from his participation at Mass. When he is in town he comes to Mass regularly, and though he is a celebrity and stands out in this regard, to me he is a parishioner like everyone else. I see how he is with people, and if someone in need approaches him, he always treats them with compassion and care.

"Martin is certainly a family man but he comes to Mass mostly by himself, though Emilio accompanies him sometimes," Fr. Kerze continues. "When there are family funerals, then the whole family comes. I know it sounds like a cliché, but Martin walks the talk; he is a man of integrity and what you see is what you get."

Father Kerze coached Martin for his role as a priest in two films. The first was the 2011 film *Stella Days*, about a rural Irish village coming into the modern era where Martin had to learn how to administer the last rites in Latin according to the pre-Vatican ritual. Kerze thinks Martin got the last rites down just fine! The second was how to celebrate Mass for the 2014 film *Trash*.

Martin's pastor remembers the Easter Vigil in 2002 when *The West Wing* was in production. After the lighting of the Easter fire and the procession to the altar with the paschal candle, the parish custom was to keep the church in darkness except for the candles. When the lights came on and Fr. Bill turned around, the entire cast of *The West Wing* was sitting in the front pews. Martin had invited them for the Easter Vigil and they all came. "It was a wonderful thing to see," said the priest.

In August of that year, Martin's beloved brother Alfonso, "Al," died. Al had never married and was a machinist at NCR in Dayton and at Honeywell in California. The entire cast of *The West Wing* came for the funeral. Father Kerze recalls sitting with Allison Janney, who played C. J. Cregg, and Richard Schiff, who played Toby Ziegler, at the reception after the Mass.

Father Kerze also remembers how interesting life became for him during *The West Wing* years, when various bishops across the country would contact him. They wanted him, as Martin's pastor, to do them a "favor" and somehow get Martin to come and speak in their dioceses. "I carried a card with his manager's phone number on it in my pocket and was always happy to pass it on, but this did not always please their excellencies. I explained that I was the pastor, not an agent, but they had a hard time grasping that it would not be appropriate for me to broker speaking engagements for a parishioner. They weren't always happy with me," said Fr. Bill with a smile.

This book opens with Martin Sheen's memory of his First Holy Communion, when he received the Eucharist for the first time. Now, sixty-five years later, his understanding of the Eucharist transcends his childhood experience. Martin views the Eucharist and community together as the key to how he sees the world. He is grateful for what he has learned about community from people like Daniel Berrigan, Phil Berrigan, and the Catholic Workers in New York and Los Angeles. He loves the Mass. "I am still astonished at the gift of the Eucharist," he says. "How are we able to receive the Body and Blood of Jesus? How is it possible? How can we even conceive of such a thing? When I get in line for Communion, wherever I am, I just say to God, 'I'm with them, whoever they are. I'm going with them, wherever they are going, count me in.' "

Mary is Martin's favorite saint, and he loves to give rosaries to people. Behind his home in Malibu there is a circular swimming pool that his grandchildren love. In the middle, on a patch of earth, is a modest statue of the Blessed Virgin. At the back of the property is a worn basketball court where he keeps a rosary and where he spends quiet time shooting hoops and then praying the rosary. He prays for someone by name on each bead.

There are crosses in his home, and all kinds of crucifixes and crosses hang on the back wall of the closet of his office. On the door hangs a ceramic sign "Deo Gratias." Martin explained that so many people give him crosses, that he cannot even display them all. "They are very personal," he explains. "Some," he says with reverence, "are from people in El Salvador." The reason he keeps "Deo Gratias" (Thanks be to God) displayed is because it is on Dorothy Day's headstone on her grave and reflects his own profound attitude of thankfulness. In another room is a beautiful composite image of Cesar Chavez by Octavio Ocampo, made up of faces of people; Martin's is among them.

"I love the journey," Martin said when asked about the spiritual life. "I am always nervous on airplanes so whenever I would get on a plane I'd bargain with God: Get us a safe landing, and I'll do this or that. Even when I came back to the church I'd get my rosary out because I was afraid.

"Once when I was on a plane leaving Washington, DC, I was just exhausted. I was the first one on the plane and I fell fast asleep as soon as I took my seat. All of a sudden I was jolted awake. I had no time to get out my rosary, so I told God: Thank you for this life; it's been wonderful. I could not have asked for anything better. If I don't make it back, be with those I leave behind. If this is the end of the journey, it's been wonderful and I am grateful.

"Even this horrible time this year with our son [Charlie Sheen], it has made us, my wife and me and our family, pray more fervently. I love Julian of Norwich and St. Therese who said: 'Everything is grace.' This is what my life is, through all the anger, everything: grace."[2]

Family

As for being a parent in Hollywood, Martin said in October 2011: "There are no criteria, there's no code to being a father in Hollywood. It's all happenstance; there is no way you can predict or prepare or plan for such energy that emanates out of this place. Charlie is going through what I went through on my journey. Charlie has practical experience about trust. He is a loving, deeply sensitive man trying to find his way in a very dark corridor. We, his parents, will be waiting at the end of that corridor with a lit candle."[3]

"Our children come through us. They're ours . . . they're ours to care for. You can only love your children by letting them go . . . having enough faith to trust that the real freedom of love will bring them back."[4]

Martin and Janet maintain an open door policy for their children and grandchildren. The Malibu family home, which he and Janet have maintained for more than forty years, is open to them all. However, there is a rule that when the grandchildren come over, it is their time. If their parents have anything to discuss between them, they are to do it elsewhere.

Joe Estevez, Martin's youngest brother, is closest to his brother John in age and friendship. If you are not paying attention you will think it is Martin passing by but it will turn out to be Joe—they resemble one another that much. Joe wanted to follow in Martin's footsteps from the time he was a kid, as he narrates in his book *Joe Estevez: Wiping off the Sheen.*[5] In an interview Joe told me that [Martin] "was my idol, and he was incredibly charismatic. He was my father's favorite son, though he would deny it. I don't recall him ever getting a thrashing. . . . My father had shotguns, and he would go hunting for rabbits every November with Martin—and they actually shot some. I would have loved to have gone with them."

After a stint in the navy, and then married with a child, Joe tried Los Angeles but could not get a foothold. He tried being a singer and admits, "I was a terrible!" In 1974 Martin, who already had the lead in *The Story of Pretty Boy Floyd*, got Joe an interview with writer and director Clyde Ware for a part, which he got. Joe says that was the last time his brother ever gave him a leg up. Everything else (more than 250 roles in mostly B movies), Joe has achieved himself.

Unfortunately, other than the acting bug, the one thing the brothers had in common was alcohol, especially during the 1970s when both were trying to forge their careers. Both showed up drunk on the set of *Apocalypse Now* (though not at the same time), and it makes one wonder if this addiction got in the way of their relationship. Public drunken behavior is a threat to making it in Hollywood. Thankfully, both have come through that dark night and today are in recovery and are practicing Catholics. Joe says that he loves his brother, but they are not really friends.

Like every family on the earth, Martin's intergenerational family is a work in progress.

In 2003 the Estevez siblings were visiting family in Ireland when they got the news that their brother Carlos, a recovering alcoholic and heavy smoker, was diagnosed with lung cancer. He died in Brownsville, Texas, in 2010. Carlos had been in the merchant marines and traveled the world but his most memorable job was training and grooming horses. "He was the only one in the family," Frank said, "who had anything to do with horses other than betting on them. He loved to watch the horses run the track at Churchill Downs when he worked there for a couple of years. He lived on Social Security, didn't have a car, television, or phone, and he died happy."

With heart and humor

Family, spirituality, and activism are not dour things to Martin. The nonviolent activists he knows are filled with joy, and he is, too.

> I love to ponder the mystery of God's presence in the world, this huge demented inn that has no room for him, yet Christ comes, uninvited. Think of it—how much God loves us, to come uninvited.
>
> I get so distracted at Mass sometimes, thinking about a million different things, and then I hear, "Behold the Lamb of God who takes away the sins of the world." Just think about that for a moment. We say this three times, and this includes the sins of the worst people in history, and my sins. The invitation is so overwhelming, to "Behold the Lamb of God." When I focus on this, I know that the world is still okay somehow, because of the sacrifice of Christ. His is the one presence we can count on, because it has meaning and brings such joy to our lives. I count on the sacraments for joy. This is the only word I can use.

Receiving the sacraments is such a joyful experience. I just give thanks and praise. That's all I can do. I am just so happy to be alive.

Martin loves the quote that he attributes to Richard Rohr, OFM, "We don't go to heaven; we become heaven." He shared this with his friend Ethel Kennedy one day when they were having dinner, and she said emphatically, "Oh no, no, no! I am going to heaven!" "She believes she will see her husband Bobby in heaven, and this is her focus," daughter Rory Kennedy told Martin. Ethel has told Martin many stories about Bobby, but especially how he changed when he realized how distant he was from the poor. When at the peace conference in Oslo in 2013, Martin quoted part of Bobby's famous 1966 Cape Town "ripple of hope" speech. When Robert Kennedy gave that speech, Nelson Mandela, who would become the first black president of South Africa in 1994, was imprisoned four miles away on Robben Island.

Nelson Mandela is another of Martin's heroes. Martin saw *Mandela: Long Walk to Freedom* and said, "I am so proud that the filmmakers got it right."

When talking with Martin, a funny story is bound to make its way into the conversation soon enough. For example, Martin tells about being in Paris in May 1990. Charlie had called and invited his parents to Cannes where he would be promoting a film. He offered them a ride back to Los Angeles with him on the studio jet. So Martin and Janet rented a car and drove from Paris to Cannes. Martin tells the story:

People kept telling us where to stop along the way but I only wanted to go to Lourdes. Janet was not interested but as we got closer and closer, I showed her the map. "We're so close; maybe we can just go for the day? We won't stay."

She agreed so we parked and walked around the shrine at Lourdes. I told her I would be at the grotto because I just wanted to pray. I got in line with the other pilgrims to walk through the grotto where the spring is and said my prayers. Janet was sitting on a bench near the river, and I said, "Okay, we can go," to which she replied, "That's it?" "Yep, that's pretty much it."

Then she asked about a box that people were walking up to and dropping things in. "That's for your intentions." "What are they?" she asked. "Well, if you want a miracle in your life or have a special prayer, you write down your intention on a piece of paper and put it in the box." "Really? Anyone can do that?" "Yes," I told her, "You write down the miracle you want, your intentions, the prayer you want answered, and put it in the box near the Holy Mother." Janet said, "Give me a minute," and she began writing. I walked around for a bit but when I got back to the bench she said, "Not yet!" She's writing and writing and finally, she puts the paper into an envelope and seals it and hands it to me. I say, "Oh no! You have to take it up there, pray for the miracle, and put it in the box yourself." "Oh for heaven's sake! I can't!" "Yes, you can, and make the sign of the cross too." So she puts the envelope into her purse and joins the line. When she came back she said, "This is a nice place. Why don't we stay the night?"

We bought some souvenirs, got some Lourdes water, and noticed a rabbi in front of us, pushing a kid. He's from New York and telling the boy, "Hey, you know them miracles? Listen, they don't happen overnight. Sometimes they happen on the plane on the way home, and sometimes years later. You never know with her. You've gotta have faith, I'm telling you. That's the important thing." So I said to him, "Excuse me, Rabbi . . ." He replied, "I'm not a rabbi. I'm a Catholic priest. I had a brain tumor and had it removed. That's why I wear the yamaka, to cover the scar." (Years later, we adapted this story into Matt Clark's role as a priest in *The Way*.) The priest gave me his card but I lost contact. The boy had been in a motorcycle accident and the priest brought him to Lourdes for a cure.

Then we got a room and Janet asked, "There's a procession here tonight, right? I'd like to do that." She went and bought the candles and we walked in the rosary procession with about twenty thousand people.

We ended up taking a commercial flight home from Cannes. We were about half way across the Atlantic and had finished dinner. Janet was sitting by the window, and I was sitting on the aisle. She starts looking through her purse and then pulls out an envelope and exclaimed, "Oh no! I left the wrong envelope in Lourdes! I put the envelope with my shopping list in the box! Here's the one for the Holy Mother!"

I love to tell this story and whenever I do, Janet always says, "You'll notice we haven't wanted for anything . . ."

Martin describes the nonviolent civil disobedience protests he takes part in as marked by joy. John Dear agrees and talks about how much fun public events for justice and peace could be with Martin, "because we would celebrate life and tell hilarious stories. . . . One time, when Phil Berrigan and I were in a terrible jail in North Carolina and had barely left our cells in nine months, Martin came to see us. This big, heavy, southern prison warden brought us into his office to meet with Martin. We all laughed and told stories, and Martin disarmed the warden. Only later did we hear that when Martin left, the warden made him pose for photos with twenty-nine of his relatives who were lined up outside."

John Dear describes something very thoughtful that Martin did at his first Mass at St. Aloysius Church in Baltimore in 1993. Martin had just arrived from South Africa, where he was filming and had met Nelson Mandela. He came straight from the airport to the church. Afterward, he disappeared; no one could find him. When he arrived he presented John with a photo album of pictures he took that morning at the Mass. He had taken all these pictures and then went to a store, had them developed, and put them together in a photo album. "It was an amazing gift. That's Martin," said Dear.

Martin has supported several charities for many years and continues to do so today. He naturally moved into social activism, his public work to stop war, nuclear weapons, and injustice. He sees all this work as part of his faith in God and discipleship to Jesus. He loves to quote the Jesuit Pierre Teilhard de Chardin: "Someday, after mastering the winds, the waves, the tides and gravity, we shall harness for God the energies of love, and then, for a second time in the history of the world, man will have discovered fire."[6]

"We are always becoming something new," Martin says. "I am reminded that everyday I am going to do a new thing, everything is going to be made new, so I don't get stuck in the past. When we are stuck in our behaviors, our past and resentments, our faults and our ego, we cannot see, we cannot move forward."

"People don't have any idea how important his faith is to him," says his friend, Fr. Michael Kennedy, SJ, "that it comes before everything. He reads so much on spirituality. He's not fake; he's totally committed."

Kennedy, who heads the Jesuit Restorative Justice Initiative in Culver City, California, also works in prison ministry in Los Angeles and is a chaplain at a juvenile hall. He has been arrested and has known Martin since 1984 when he was an associate pastor at Our Lady Queen of Angels Church, known as La Placita. Kennedy officiated at Charlie Sheen's wedding to Denise Richards in 2002.

Former US Ambassador to Malta, Douglas Kmiec, Fr. Kerze, and Fr. Michael Kennedy all speak about Martin's friendship with the late Monsignor John Sheridan (1916–2010), who had been Martin's confessor for many years. Father Kerze remembers gathering in the monsignor's room after Mass on a Saturday evening where Martin would be visiting, telling stories, and laughing. Kennedy recalls how deep the spiritual connection was between the aged priest and the actor, and how Sheridan was a model of holiness for Martin. Although Msgr. Sheridan was always Martin's first choice when a priest was needed for an episode of *The West Wing*, Fr. Kennedy appeared twice on the show. When Doug Kmiec and Martin get together and share stories about people who have drifted in and out of their lives, "Msgr. Sheridan figures prominently because he was a larger than life figure, and his voice can still be so readily heard when we remember him," according to Fr. Kerze.

In the foreword to Ambassador Doug Kmiec's 2012 remarkable memoir, *Lift Up Your Hearts*, Martin writes about the death of Msgr. Sheridan in 2010:

> In the early afternoon of August 25, 2010, as my son Emilio and I were driving east through Malibu Canyon, we learned that three dear and close friends had been involved in a terrible accident on nearby Mulholland Highway. We turned around immediately and arrived at the scene about an hour after the accident, to discover that Sr. Mary Campbell had been killed instantly, and that Msgr. John Sheridan and Doug Kmiec, the driver, had been taken to UCLA Medical Center, both in critical condition. Thus began a long and steep spiral into the depths of personal grief, guilt, depression accompanied by unimagined suffering for Doug. . . ."[7]

The three friends were returning from the sixtieth anniversary celebration at the Catholic Louisville High School in Woodland Hills, California, when the rental car Doug was driving apparently skid on gravel and turned over. Sister Mary died at the scene and Msgr. Sheridan died three weeks later on September 17.

As Martin looked around the accident site, he saw the body of his friend, Sr. Mary, a sister of St. Louis, covered with a sheet. He started to walk toward her. A policeman stopped him saying he could not go any further. But Martin had reached in his pocket for a rosary and holding it out told the officer said, "I know Sr. Mary, and I would like to put a rosary in her hand." The officer stood aside and allowed him to pass.

The day of the accident was Fr. Bill Kerze's day off but he returned to the parish as soon as he heard the news. He recalls that Martin came directly to the office to find out the address of Sr. Brigid McGuigan, RSC, who served there with Sr. Mary. He wanted to go there to tell her personally about what had happened so she wouldn't have to hear it from strangers. Ambassador Kmiec remembered them in an interview:

> We lost two brilliant teachers and lovely souls, Msgr. Sheridan and Sr. Mary Campbell, whom Martin and I counted as our best friends. Of course, these best friends had led truly extraordinary lives, and they made everyone feel as if they were their best friends. The tragedy is a horrible memory. It has tested my faith; it has destroyed the faith of others. And yet, Martin has found a way to help me realize the redemptive grace of suffering and the goodness and the empathy that is born of it.
>
> On the day of Monsignor John's funeral, I was still weak from my own surgeries from which I had not yet recovered. I was mortified by the thought of saying farewell. And I was worried that the accident had so severely injured my relationship with the parish that I would have to move somewhere

else. Martin sensed all this, and embraced me, and like Christ on the way to Calvary, invited me to help carry the casket, as a definitive statement of love and inclusion.

Is Martin a humanitarian? Of course he is, but not in a way that suggests a plaque, but as someone holding a ladle and serving soup or perhaps holding a spoon that feeds the man who is too weak to feed himself.

When I was the Ambassador to Malta, I invited Martin to visit. I thought this would draw attention to the work we were doing on behalf of the irregular migrant travelers across the treacherous Mediterranean who ended up either in Lampedusa, Italy, or Malta. I convinced the then Secretary of State, [Hillary] Clinton, to allow an increased level of resettlement in the United States. In order to get this accomplished, however, I had to find outside resources. Martin, and his son, Emilio Estevez, quite generously agreed to travel to Malta on February 28, 2011, for the European premiere of the film *The Way* as a charity event. Significant sums were raised for the Pope John XXIII Peace Lab and the care of these people.

In November 2014 a film by Jeremy Culver and narrated by Martin Sheen was released: *The Radical Kindness of Monsignor John Sheridan*.

Along the Way

In 1999, a homeless man named David Duval was down and out and living on the streets in Santa Monica because he loved the ocean. He went to the 6:00 a.m. Mass each morning at St. Monica's Church and would often stay afterwards to sit and pray.

One morning, as David was walking out of the church, he saw a man kneeling in prayer who looked very familiar. He recognized Martin Sheen, who looked up at him. "You are here so often," Martin said. David replied, "I've never seen you here before." Then Martin said, "If you have a minute I would love to talk to you."

"I told him I was homeless," recalls Duval. "I am sure things will work out for you," Martin said. "Why don't you come back tomorrow and meet me here?"

The next day Martin gave David a check for $1,500, a silver cross, and a letter from the "Office of the Acting President of the West Wing." David continued telling his story through tears, "Since that time, fifteen years ago, I've gotten married and have an eleven-year-old daughter. I manage several properties and am involved with some music groups. All I can say is that it is because of people like Martin that I am sitting here, talking to you today. Of everyone I know on the planet, Martin Sheen is the one person I would hold up as being the best human you can be. He's just amazing."

The five-time Emmy Award-winning producer Terrance "Terry" Sweeney, whom Martin worked with on the *Insight* series, is the executive producer for *Bhopal: A Prayer for Rain*, starring Martin, Mischa Barton, and Kal Penn. It is an independent feature, and as with many independent films, it took several years to make. *Bhopal* is about the 1984 Union Carbide cyanide gas leak at their plant in Bhopal, India. This tragedy caused more than 15,000 deaths and 550,000 injuries. Sweeney writes:

> Martin's courage saved the entire production from collapse. When principal photography was about to commence, terrorists attacked the Taj Hotel in Mumbai on November 28, 2008, killing 164 people and wounding more than 600 others. Since Mumbai was the hub for international flights to our production, actors from London and the United States wanted to pull out of the film, fearing for their safety. Martin's agent and his wife, Janet, expressed their serious concerns. But Martin insisted on going forward with the filming as scheduled, in spite of the risks.

Martin's presence on location in India, in the face of exceptionally difficult production challenges, was nothing short of inspiring. He encouraged his fellow actors and the entire crew and befriended the many curious children looking on with smiles, treats and even pocket money.

I have such an appreciation for Martin on so many levels. He is as extraordinarily talented, generous, compassionate, and wholeheartedly dedicated to his family, his faith, and to making the world a better place in whatever way he can. Martin is a life force, and those who come into his universe are, indeed, blessed.

Through one of Martin's co-actors in *Bhopal*, Vasanth Santosham, Martin learned about a program called Native Vision. Vasanth's father, Dr. Mathu Santosham, is the director of the program through the Johns Hopkins Center for American Indian Health in Baltimore. In 2013 Martin and Vasanth spent a week at the Native Vision Sports and Life Skills Camp in Shiprock, New Mexico, to teach acting to young people. At the end, Martin took part in a skit with them called "Navajo News," about comic moments in Navajo life. Martin said that the reason he became involved was because "as a nation, we've really forgotten about our Native-American population," he said. "Our citizens on the reservation have been totally neglected for so very long that we're unaware of them."[8]

Martin provides support to St. Monica School in Santa Monica and Our Lady of Malibu School in Malibu. Monsignor Torgerson of St. Monica's says that Martin's scholarship assistance makes it possible for children outside Santa Monica to attend, and this brings much social and cultural diversity to the school. Father Bill Kerze of Our Lady of Malibu says that whenever he mentions needs for the school or tuition aid, Martin always responds. Martin also assists a Catholic school run by Fr. Michael Doyle in one of Camden, New Jersey's most impoverished and troubled areas.

The West Wing

During the 1980s and '90s Martin was working continuously, in both television and film. Matt Clark says that one of the best moments and memories in his life was directing Martin Sheen in *Da* in 1988, about a New York playwright who returns to Ireland when his father dies. About his friendship with Martin, Matt says,

> I love Martin more than anyone in my life. He's a wonderful actor but I don't think of him as an actor. I think of his humanity. My connection is to his heart; it is so big, so wide, and so accepting. I can never forget the homeless man in Malibu that we would see all the time. He could barely stand up; he was dirty and he smelled. But once a month Martin would pick him up, take him to a motel, and pay for him to have a night off the streets and get cleaned up. He gives people rides and gives them money. I think they use the money for drugs, but Martin's business is humanity, trying to help.

Martin made his directorial debut in a rather predictable film titled *Cadence* (1991). It starred his sons Charlie Sheen and Ramon Estevez and Martin's friend, Matt Clark. Martin played a bigoted sergeant at a military prison in Germany in the 1960s. Charlie was one of the solider inmates with an attitude. Both had much to learn.

Gerry Straub is a secular Franciscan and a former network television producer. He gave it all up to make films that tell stories about the poor and social justice through his nonprofit, Serving the Poor through the Power of Film.[9] One Sunday he arrived early for the evening Mass at St. Charles Borromeo Church in Los Angeles. He was alone in the church and was surprised that no one else was there and then realized the Mass schedule had changed to a half hour later. Another person came in and knelt down across the aisle. When Gerry looked up he saw that it was Martin Sheen. Gerry was praying fervently for a way to move his ministry forward, especially to fund a short film project to support a larger one, a coffee-table book filled with photos of some of the poorest people on earth, called *When Did I See You Hungry?*[10] After Mass, Gerry introduced himself to Martin Sheen as they walked to the parking lot across the street and discovered they had a mutual friend, Fr. John Dear. Gerry told Martin about the project, and he agreed to narrate it during the upcoming five-week hiatus in taping episodes of *The West Wing*.

But Martin had to go to Ireland for a family matter and had to cancel all the projects he had lined up. His manager called Gerry and told him that the only project he would still do, on the one free day he had, would be *When Did I See You Hungry?*

"Martin was so charming and polite," said Gerry. "It was almost a three-hour session, and sometimes we would have to stop and discuss how to pronounce a word. When I gave in, I would say to him, 'Okay, have it your way, Mr. President.' At the break, all he talked about was Mother Teresa, and at the end of the session he asked me to autograph his copy of the script. You can imagine how that made me feel." Later, in 2008, Martin sponsored a film student from Columbia University, Nick Ellsberg, so he could travel to Uganda with Gerry as an intern. They filmed documentary footage for *The Fragrant Spirit of Life*, about the desperate, heartbreaking plight of children in impoverished, war-torn parts of Uganda.

More recently, Martin starred in *The Way* (2010), directed by his son Emilio Estevez, as well as *The Amazing Spider-Man* (2012). If you look up "Martin Sheen" on the Internet Movie Database that lists movies and television credits, you will see that he has been working nonstop since the first entry in 1961.

About a decade before *The Way*, however, came the exceptional television series, *The West Wing.*

The West Wing was must see television between 1999 and 2006 because it was time for Aaron Sorkin (as series creator and lead writer for the first four seasons) to take us to school each week. Thoughtful viewers knew that the show not only entertained but also was teaching us something at high speed, as the characters paced from room to room, snapping clever dialogue at each other. The curriculum included topics like cartography, political ethics, war, capital punishment, grief, honesty, and faith. *The West Wing* was a laboratory for questioning the political process and rhetoric. Over seven seasons the show, its writers, actors, and crew received numerous awards and nominations, including Martin. The Writers Guild of America lists *The West Wing* tenth in its list of "101 Best Written TV Shows of All Time." In 2013, *TV Guide* ranked the show in the top sixty best series of all time. Martin Sheen played President Josiah "Jed" Bartlet, a Notre Dame graduate, whose Clintonesque administration offered a contrast to the Bush White House at the time. Richard Schiff, who played Toby Ziegler, said in 2010:

> I think *The West Wing* was a perfect storm of good things in every possible way. No other political show had ever been successful. We were coming off a run of peace and prosperity, relatively, and it certainly was a prosperous time because of Bill Gates and the whole techno boom. There was a time of . . . fantasy. Also, the scandals of the Clinton

administration kind of brought our feelings about that administration to a low point. Then we came along. We were really the Clinton administration, only in Camelot.[11]

Of all the television shows Martin has been part of, *The West Wing* tops his list. His favorite episode, as already mentioned, remains "Take This Sabbath Day" (see page 94). His second favorite is "In Excelsis Deo" (season 1, episode 10). The main story line, among several, features a homeless Korean War veteran who dies alone on Washington's cold streets at Christmas, wearing a thrift store jacket. Toby Ziegler (Schiff), the White House Communication Director and Senior Domestic Policy Advisor, had donated a coat to charity, and when the police find his business card in the pocket, they call him. Toby traces the man's next of kin, and, on his own authority, arranges for a military funeral at Arlington National Cemetery. Writers Aaron Sorkin and Rick Cleveland won an Emmy for this episode and rightly so. They deftly, and movingly, contrast Toby, whose character is Jewish, with a clear understanding of the Christmas spirit in action.

Martin's number three pick is "Two Cathedrals" (season 2, episode 22). In this episode President Bartlet's beloved, truth-telling personal secretary, Mrs. Landingham (Kathryn Joosten), has died suddenly in the previous episode and now the White House staff attends her funeral at the National Cathedral. Bartlet reminisces about Mrs. Landingham, who has known him since she was his father's secretary at the prep school he attended as a teenager. After the funeral, Bartlet remains alone in the cathedral and rants, even curses God in anger—and in Latin. He cannot decide whether to run again for president. He struggles with his grief at her loss and what he knows Mrs. Landingham would tell him.

While many viewers became political science students or emotionally invested in the show, Jacques Steinberg of the *New York Times* wrote that "Martin came to liken the show's role to that of good, escapist fiction. 'In order to sometimes get a different perspective on what's going down in the world, to reach back to your humanity, you read novels,' Mr. Sheen said. 'We're like the reading of a novel.' "[12]

Martin also said, "On the show, we are not trying to get people to eat their vegetables; we are not trying to get people to become Democrats. We are basically trying to encourage people to get involved with public life so that politics isn't left to the wealthy and privileged."[13]

Elizabeth Moss who played the president's daughter, Zoey, said of working with Martin, "Any time I got to work with him, I was so honored. He was so much fun and so sweet . . . and a lot of my scenes are with him, so that was the highlight every single time."[14]

Carla Ward worked as an extra on *The West Wing* for every episode during the show's final season (2005–06.) She had just left the Air Force, and the only television show she watched was *The West Wing*. Since she was looking for something to do while she was working on her doctorate at UCLA, she answered a casting call for extras. She worked one episode and enjoyed being part of the "White House staff" so much that she asked the casting company to put her on the first call list, which they did. Carla says of Martin:

> What I first noticed about Martin was that he treated everyone equally, whether they were union or non-union, main actors, or one of the crew. He was friendly and he did not ignore people.
>
> Actors' trailers were on one side of the sound stage where we filmed at the Warner Bros. studio in Burbank. The trailers for the background extras, like me, were on

the other. So we didn't see the key actors that much, but we would see them at catering. Martin would get in line with the rest of us and sit with us to eat; he didn't hide out. I don't recall the others doing that.

The actors on *The West Wing* were good people. Other extras that had been there from the beginning told me that Martin set the tone for that early on—there would be no elitism or treating people differently.

Unrelated to her stint on *The West Wing*, Carla became a volunteer for the Office of the Americas peace organization, for which Martin serves on the board. She tells a funny story about two marches that Martin led. "He could never go two steps into a crowd without someone stopping him to chat," Carla explained. The first time that Theresa Bonpane (cofounder of the OOA) asked her to "go and collect Martin" so the march could begin, he just nodded at her and kept on chatting. At the next event, Theresa asked her again to collect Martin. Carla told her, "You know he's just going to nod, ignore me, and keep on talking." And he did. "But I love this about Martin Sheen," she said. "He made that fan, that person, feel like the most important person in the world."

Carla continued, "Now I go to Our Lady of Malibu Church, the same as Martin, and I have become friends with him and his family. I adopted a little boy, Matthew, a few months ago, and I asked Martin to be the godfather at his baptism, which he accepted. Now at Mass, when Matthew gets fussy, I hand him to Martin and he calms down right away. I am a single mom, and I am happy that Martin is in my son's life. Martin has a heart of gold."

Since his term as "The Acting President of the United States" and Honorary Mayor of Malibu ended, and after being asked to run for office with Ralph Nader for the Green

Party in 1996 and by the Democrats to run for the Senate in 2004[15] (both of which he declined), Martin doesn't do politics. But he did team up with former cast members to lobby for legislation in real life. On March 31, 2009, Bradley Whitford (Josh Lyman, deputy chief of staff), and Richard Schiff, (Toby) lobbied on Capitol Hill for the Employee Free Choice Act that would make it easier for workers to unionize.

"I am not a politician or a public servant," Martin said. "I am still a journeyman actor and a peace and justice activist. I'm a pilgrim trying to win my freedom and serve as best I can in the time I have, with this gift I've been given."[16]

To a newspaper in England he said, "Acting is what I do for a living," he added. "Activism is what I do to stay alive."[17]

Notre Dame at Last

On March 1, 2008, Notre Dame University announced that on May 18 it would bestow its prestigious Laetare Medal, the highest Catholic award in the United States, to Martin Sheen. Previous recipients include the actress Irene Dunne and the diplomat, Clare Booth Luce, as well as some of Martin's heroes: President John F. Kennedy, Dorothy Day, Cardinal Joseph Bernardin, and fellow death penalty abolitionist, Sr. Helen Prejean, CSJ. The Laetare Medal was instituted at Notre Dame in 1883. The recipient is announced on the Fourth Sunday of Lent, Laetare Sunday, when the church takes a respite during the solemn penitential Lenten season to celebrate joy. The award was envisioned as the American version of a papal honor called the "Golden Rose" that predates the eleventh century: "The medal has been awarded annually at Notre Dame to a Catholic whose genius has ennobled the arts and sciences, illustrated the ideals of the Church and enriched the heritage of humanity."

The day before Martin received the Laetare Medal, he spoke to about 160 Notre Dame graduates at the Senior Service Send-Off Ceremony before they left to go abroad for a year of service:

> You will often remain uncompensated for your time and talent, and your behavior may be acceptable only to a precious few. But your loyalty and values will never be subject to compromise. You may live a happy and even productive life. And though you won't leave much of an inheritance, you will leave a substantial legacy of social justice, and be a great source of spiritual nourishment for those who may choose to follow.[18]

In his eloquent acceptance remarks on May 17, Martin first expressed his gratitude for now having an actual connection to Notre Dame University, rather than the pretend one he had when he was President Bartlet on *The West Wing*. He joked, "Now we are stuck with each other!"

Martin then neatly transitioned into talking about what drives him: our responsibility for one another.

> Surely, [it is] a lofty ideal as rare in a culture of so many compromised values and so much cynicism, a culture that all too often knows the price of everything and the value of nothing. Yet, there remains a very real and mysterious yearning, deep within each and every human heart that compels us to journey outside of ourselves by descending deeper within. Yet this inadvertent root must be built to the specifications of the individual heart, and the cost is high. If it were not so, we would be left to question its value. For some of us in this journey it may be a natural progression, for some it may be a sudden shift, for some it may be the result of a near-death experience, or a dead-end realization. For some, it may be less a journey than a pilgrimage.

It does not matter how we define it or when it begins, but it is absolutely essential that it continue, because it is only here we can come to know ourselves, in deeply revealing ways that confirm our worth and define our purpose. It is here where we are forced to acknowledge our powerlessness, and where we begin to realize how truly powerful we are. It is here where the ego befriends the truth, and we are free to visualize the very first small, conscious acts of heroism, that bring rejection from the crowd and satisfaction from the heart. And it is here into this world, this demented end, where there is absolutely no room for Him at all, that Christ comes uninvited to lift us up, and set us on the path that will unite the will of the spirit to the work of the flesh.[19]

Conclusion

Martin Sheen is not a complicated man but he is a man of depth. He loves acting and has worked nonstop since the early 1960s in films, plays, and television. He loves his wife, children, and family. He is a devout Catholic who attends Mass regularly, practices his faith, and stays very involved in the movement for disarmament, justice, and peace. Combined with this outgoing, generous spirit, these characteristics have made him one of the most beloved figures of our time.

In 2009 Emilio directed his father in what has become a spiritual classic, *The Way*. It has an implicit theme of thankfulness that is gradually revealed. Making *The Way* was a family affair: Martin and Janet were executive producers, grandson Tyler was an associate producer, Renée plays the doctor's assistant, and Martin's friend Matt Clark plays a priest who wears a yamaka to cover up a scar on his head from cancer surgery.

The Way, the Camino, is about a father, Dr. Tom Avery, who impulsively decides to carry his dead son Daniel's ashes along the five hundred mile Camino de Santiago de Compostela in Spain. Daniel played by Emilio, tells his disapproving father as he leaves Los Angeles for his journey where he will die suddenly, "You don't choose a life, Dad. You live one." Tom is unprepared to be changed by the grace of the pilgrimage, to admit that he can learn something from his son. He is just as unprepared for the community he forms with three other pilgrims, as they trek the medieval pilgrim path together, at times harsh, at other times almost whimsical. Tom is an eye doctor who thinks he can see everything as it is, but only begins to see clearly and experience life for the first time while on the Camino. Catholics in Media Associates in Los Angeles gave *The Way* its film award in 2011.

Their memoir, *Along the Way*, traces Martin and Emilio's real life journey, framed by the making of this film together.

This brief biography seeks to shed light on the arc of one man's journey to follow Jesus in this life and make a difference. As Martin mentioned in an interview:

> All the people who have made a difference in the human race, paid attention to and lived in the times in which they were born. As Christ, all the great prophets, martyrs, saints, heroes, lived in their own times, so we are called to be present to the times in which we live. This motivates me to remember that I won't be here for my grandchildren's future. I have to live *now*. So I think about the injustices in the world, war, and the environment. I can only speak to the time in which I live and this motivates who I am and what I do.

Notes

Introduction—pages 1–4

1. Martin Sheen and Emilio Estevez, *Along the Way: The Journey of a Father and Son* (New York: Free Press, 2012).

2. Jeff Dietrich, *Broken and Shared: Food, Dignity, and the Poor on Los Angeles' Skid Row* (Los Angeles: Marymount Institute Press, 2011), xvii.

3. David Kupfer, "Martin Sheen Interview," *The Progressive*, June 30, 2003, http://www.progressive.org/news/2003/06/1155/martin -sheen-interview#sthash.vibKzUvd.dpuf.

Chapter One: The Pilgrimage Begins—pages 5–19

1. Sheen, Martin, interview with James Lipton, *Inside the Actors Studio*, Bravo, August 10, 2003, as quoted in "The True Identity of Charlie Sheen: Tracing the Roots of the Estevez Family" by Erika Ramirez. February 28, 2011. http://www.latina.com/entertainment /buzz/true-identity-charlie-sheen-tracing-roots-Estevez-family.

2. Chaminade High School and Julienne High School merged to become Chaminade Julienne Catholic High School in 1973. http:// www.cjeagles.org/about-cj/history-cj.

3. Sheen and Estevez, *Along the Way*, 30.

4. Sheila Flynn, "Martin Sheen, the 'President' at School," *The Washington Post*, December 7, 2006. http://www.washingtonpost .com/wp-dyn/content/article/2006/12/07/AR2006120701049.html.

Chapter Two: An Actor on the Way—pages 20–36

1. Dotson Radner, "I Discovered What Faith and Love Are Really About," *Parade*, December 2, 2001, 4–6.

2. Jim Hargrove, *Martin Sheen: Actor and Activist* (Chicago: Children's Press, 1991), cf. chap. 3.

3. Hargrove, *Martin Sheen*, 29.

4. Kupfer, "Martin Sheen Interview."

5. The best list of all Martin Sheen's films and television shows is under his name on the Internet Movie Database, http://imdb.com.

6. Lee Riley and David Shumacher, *The Sheens: Martin, Charlie and Emilio Estevez* (London: Robson Books, 1991), 52. [Martin Sheen stressed to the author that this book is completely unauthorized, however he agreed that this unreferenced quote does reflect his views on awards.]

7. Sheen and Estevez, *Along the Way*, 48–54.

8. Hargrove, *Martin Sheen*, 41.

9. Sheen and Estevez, *Along the Way*, 62.

10. Ibid., 64–65.

11. Ibid., 62–67.

12. Ibid., 62–63.

13. The Humanitas Prize was established by Paulist priest Fr. Ellwood "Bud" Kieser in 1974 to honor film and television writers "who affirm the human dignity, explore the meaning of life, enlighten the use of human freedom and reveal to each person our common humanity." http://humanitas prize.org.

14. Martin narrated the documentary about the iconic actor *James Dean: Forever Young* in 2005.

15. Sheen and Estevez, *Along the Way*, 126–7.

16. Ibid., 126–7.

17. Ryan Gilbey, "The Start of Something Beautiful," *The Guardian*, August 21, 2008, http://www.theguardian.com/film/2008/aug/22/drama.

18. Hargrove, *Martin Sheen*, 49–50.

Chapter Three: Spiritual Journey—pages 37–56

1. The source for information and quotes about Martin Sheen and the *Insight* series is based on an unpublished memoir that Michael Rhodes graciously prepared as a source for this book.

2. Rose Pacatte, "On the Way with Martin Sheen," *National Catholic Reporter*, October 7, 2011, http://ncronline.org/news /spirituality/way-martin-sheen.

3. *Dialogue on Film*: "Filmmaker Emile de Antonio talks with the actor about *Gandhi* and *Apocalypse Now,* plus their new film about the Berrigan brothers," December 1982, transcribed from an audio recording, http://vonne920.tripod.com/martin_sheen/ms _dialogue.html.

4. Joe Estevez, Brad Paulson, and Chris Watson, *Joe Estevez: Wiping Off the Sheen* (Duncan, OK: Bear Manor Media, 2012), 52.

5. Hargrove, *Martin Sheen,* 75–76.

6. Sheen and Estevez, *Along the Way,* 259ff.

7. Ibid., 271.

8. Ibid., 270.

9. Rebecca Cusey, "Martin Sheen talks about his Golden Anniversary with Wife Janet" *Patheos: Tinsel Town*, December, 22, 2011, http://www.patheos.com/blogs/tinseltalk/2011/12/martin-sheen-talks -about-his-golden-anniversary-with-wife-janet.

10. Pacatte, "On the Way with Martin Sheen."

11. Sean Romer, "The Traditional Catholic and Twelve Step Programs," September 2002, http://www.angelusonline.org/index.php ?section=articles&subsection=show_article&article_id=2155.

Chapter Four: A Catholic Activist—pages 57–98

1. Howard Thompson, "The Screen: 'In the Year of the Pig' Documentary, Bows," *New York Times*, November 11, 1969, http://www .nytimes.com/movie/review?res=9B02E1DA153DEF34BC4952DFB 7678382679EDE.

2. Ricardo Yanez, email message to author, August 1, 2014. Information is from the unpublished archives of the International Catholic Organization for Cinema (OCIC) Brussels, Belgium. OCIC merged with Unda World (International Catholic Association for Television

and Radio) to become SIGNIS, the international Catholic organization for communication in 2002. http://signis.net.

3. Erik Gardner, "Ed Asner's SAG-AFTRA Lawsuit Dismissed," *The Hollywood Reporter*, January 29, 2014, http://www.hollywoodreporter.com/thr-esq/ed-asners-sag-aftra-lawsuit-675376.

4. "Actor Sheen Seized in Protest," *Los Angeles Times*, June, 20, 1986, http://articles.latimes.com/1986-06-20/news/mn-11623_1_defense-contracts.

5. Robert Lindsey, "438 Protesters Are Arrested at Nevada Nuclear Test Site," *New York Times*, February 6, 1987, http://www.nytimes.com/1987/02/06/us/438-protesters-are-arrested-at-nevada-nuclear-test-site.html.

6. Charles Champlin, "The Committed Life of Martin Sheen," *Los Angeles Times*, May 19, 1988, http://articles.latimes.com/1988-05-19/entertainment/ca-4738_1_martin-sheen.

7. Ibid.

8. John Dear, "Remembering the Jesuit Martyrs," *On the Road to Peace* (blog), *National Catholic Reporter*, November 10, 2009, http://ncronline.org/blogs/road-peace/remembering-jesuit-martyrs.

9. John Dear, "Speaking for Peace with Martin Sheen in Norway," *On the Road to Peace* (blog), *National Catholic Reporter*, March 5, 2013, http://ncronline.org/blogs/road-peace/speaking-peace-martin-sheen-norway.

10. Patt Morrison, "Protesters Hold Die-In, Say 'Have a Nice Day': El Salvador: Morning routine at Federal Building stresses the *civil* in disobedience," *Los Angeles Times,* January 18, 1990, http://articles.latimes.com/1990-01-18/local/me-443_1_el-salvador.

11. E. Stoller Torrey, "Ronald Reagan's shameful legacy: Violence, the homeless, mental illness," *Salon*, September 29, 2013, http://www.salon.com/2013/09/29/ronald_reagans_shameful_legacy_violence_the_homeless_mental_illness.

12. *New York Times,* "Chilly night on a sidewalk teaches lessons about homeless," March 5, 1987, http://www.nytimes.com/1987/03/05/us/chilly-night-on-a-sidewalk-grate-teaches-lesson-about-homeless.html.

13. "Martin Sheen Meets Cesar Chavez, 'Cesar's Last Fast,'" posted by Cesar's Last Fast, October 18, 2009, https://www.youtube.com/watch?v=Ah34vjefwzQ.

14. Associated Press, "Malibu Keeping Sheen as Honorary Mayor," *New York Times*, June 12, 1989, http://www.nytimes.com/1989/06/12/us/malibu-keeping-sheen-as-honorary-mayor.html.

15. Roy Bourgeois was dismissed from the Maryknoll Society, laicized, and excommunicated for his support of women's ordination in 2012.

16. Ron Schmidt, *On the Line*, documentary film directed by Jason Schmidt and Peter Glenn, December 2nd Productions, 2007.

17. Floyd D. Spence National Defense Authorization Act for 2001, http://www.dod.mil/dodgc/olc/docs/2001NDAA.pdf.

18. United Nations Truth Commission on El Salvador, "Report of the Commission on the Truth for El Salvador," April 1, 1993, http://www.derechos.org/nizkor/salvador/informes/truth.html.

19. "Thousands Protest 'School of the Assassins,'" CNN, November 28, 1998, http://www.cnn.com/US/9811/22/americas.protest/.

20. United Nations Truth Commission on El Salvador, "Report of the Commission."

21. Sheen, foreword to *Disturbing the Peace: The Story of Roy Bourgeois and the Movement to Close the School of the Americas*, by James Hodge and Linda Cooper (Maryknoll, NY: Orbis, 2004), ix.

22. Schmidt, *On the Line*.

23. Craig Kielburger, "Martin Sheen on Mother Teresa," posted by Free the Children International, August 8, 2011, https://www.youtube.com/watch?v=54e7mOUt8js.

24. Nenad N. Bach, "Martin Sheen unveiled first monument honouring Mother Teresa," Crown: Croatian News Network, June 24, 2002, http://www.croatia.org/crown/articles/5592/1/E-Martin-Sheen-unveiled-first-monument-honouring-Mother-Teresa.html.

25. Joseph L. Bernardin, "A Consistent Ethic of Life," Gannon Lecture, Fordham University, December 6, 1983, in *The Seamless Garment: Writings on the Consistent Ethic of Life* (Maryknoll, NY: Orbis, 2008), 7–14.

26. Sheen, telephone interview with the author, August 18, 2014.

27. Mike Farrell, *Just Call Me Mike: A Journey to Actor and Activist* (New York: Akashic Books, 2008), 14–15.

28. "Yes on 34—Official TV advertisement, narrated by Martin Sheen," uploaded by Safe California's Channel, October 22, 2012, https://www.youtube.com/watch?v=txD6C9lw7gY.

29. "Martin Sheen: Latino Man Wrongly Convicted of Murder," *Fox News Latino*, December 6, 2011, http://latino.foxnews.com /latino/entertainment/2011/12/06/martin-sheen-latino-man-wrongly -convicted-murder.

30. Craig Reishus, "Martin Sheen," The Nuclear Free Future Award, http://www.nuclear-free-future.com/en/award-presentation /laureates/martin-sheen.

31. David Kupfer, "Martin Sheen Interview."

32. Reishus, "Martin Sheen."

33. Sheen, Martin, letter accepting the Nuclear Free Future Award, September 29, 2010, http://www.nuclear-free-future.com/fileadmin /user_upload/2013/martin_sheen_Letter.pdf.

Chapter Five: Spirituality of an Activated Catholic— pages 99–124

1. Nancy Frazier O'Brien, "Use of new Roman Missal to begin in US at Advent 2011," Catholic News Service, August 20, 2010, http:// www.catholicnews.com/data/stories/cns/1003382.htm.

2. Rose Pacatte, "On the Way with Martin Sheen."

3. Ibid.

4. From an interview with Martin Sheen on CNN, 1990, transcribed at http://vonne920.tripod.com/martin_sheen/estevezkids.html.

5. Estevez, Paulson, and Watson, *Joe Estevez.*

6. Adapted from Pierre Teilhard de Chardin, "The Evolution of Chastity," in *Toward the Future,* trans. René Hague (New York: Harcourt, 1936): 86–87.

7. Martin Sheen, foreword to *Lift Up Your Hearts: A True Story of Loving Your Enemies, Killing Your Friends, and the Life that Remains,* by Douglas W. Kmiec (Embassy International Press, 2012).

8. "Martin Sheen Teaches Acting to Navajo Youth at Shiprock," *Indian Country Today Media Network,* June 3, 2013, http://indian

countrytodaymedianetwork.com/2013/06/03/martin-sheen-teaches
-acting-navajo-youth-shiprock-149689.

9. Formerly called "The San Damiano Foundation."

10. Gerry Straub, *When Did I See You Hungry?* (Cincinnati: St. Anthony Messenger Press, 2002).

11. Richard Schiff, interview with Stephen J. Abramson, *The Archive of American Television*, June 3, 2010, http://www.emmytv legends.org/interviews/people/richard-schiff.

12. Jacques Steinberg, "'West Wing' Writers' Novel Way of Picking the President," *New York Times*, April 10, 2006, http://www .nytimes.com/2006/04/10/arts/television/10wing.html?module=Sear ch&mabReward=relbias%3Ar%2C%7B%221%22%3A%22RI% 3A10%22%7D

13. Kupfer, "Martin Sheen Interview."

14. Bryn Elise Sandberg, "'The West Wing' Cast Reflects on Favorite Episodes," *The Hollywood Reporter*, May 13, 2014, http:// www.hollywoodreporter.com/live-feed/west-wing-cast-reflects-favor ite-702950.

15. *BBC News,* "West Wing Star Says No to Politics," May 6, 2009, http://news.bbc.co.uk/2/hi/uk_news/politics/8037001.stm.

16. Kupfer, "Martin Sheen Interview."

17. *BBC News,* "West Wing Star Says No to Politics."

18. Michael O. Garvey, "Faith and Works at Notre Dame," *Notre Dame News*, May 29, 2008, http://news.nd.edu/news/9501-faith-and -works-at-notre-dame.

19. Martin Sheen, "Martin Sheen Laetare Acceptance Speech," *Notre Dame News*, May 17, 2008, http://news.nd.edu/news/9492 -martin-sheen-laetare-medal-acceptance-speech.

Bibliography

Print

Bernardin, Joseph L. *The Seamless Garment: Writings on the Consistent Ethic of Life.* Maryknoll, NY: Orbis, 2008.

Champlin, Charles. "The Committed Life of Martin Sheen." *Los Angeles Times* (May 19, 1988). http://articles.latimes.com/1988-05-19/entertainment/ca-4738_1_martin-sheen.

Cusey, Rebecca. "Martin Sheen talks about his Golden Anniversary with Wife Janet." *Patheos: Tinsel Town* (December, 22, 2011). http://www.patheos.com/blogs/tinseltalk/2011/12/martin-sheen-talks-about-his-golden-anniversary-with-wife-janet.

Dear, John. *A Persistent Peace: One Man's Struggle for a Nonviolent World.* Chicago: Loyola, 2008.

————. *On the Road to Peace* (blog). http://ncronline.org/blogs/road-peace.

Dietrich, Jeff. *Broken and Shared: Food, Dignity, and the Poor on Los Angeles' Skid Row.* Los Angeles: Marymount Institute, 2011.

Estevez, Joe, Brad Paulson, and Chris Watson, *Joe Estevez: Wiping Off the Sheen.* Duncan, OK: Bear Manor Media, 2012.

Farrell, Mike. *Just Call Me Mike: A Journey to Actor and Activist.* New York: Akashic Books, 2008.

Flynn, Sheila. "Martin Sheen, the 'President' at School." *The Washington Post* (December 7, 2006). http://www.washingtonpost.com/wp-dyn/content/article/2006/12/07/AR2006120701049.html.

Hargrove, Jim. *Martin Sheen: Actor and Activist*. Chicago: Children's Press, 1991.

Hodge, James, and Linda Cooper. *Disturbing the Peace: The Story of Father Roy Bourgeois and the Movement to Close the School of the Americas*. Maryknoll, NY: Orbis, 2004.

Kmiec, Douglas W. *Lift Up Your Hearts: A True Story of Loving Your Enemies, Killing Your Friends, and the Life that Remains*. Embassy International Press, 2012.

Pacatte, Rose. "On the Way with Martin Sheen." *National Catholic Reporter* (October 7, 2011). http://ncronline.org/news/spirituality/way-martin-sheen.

Ramirez, Erika. "The True Identity of Charlie Sheen: Tracing the Roots of the Estevez Family." February 28, 2011. http://www.latina.com/entertainment/buzz/true-identity-charlie-sheen-tracing-roots-Estevez-family.

Riley, Lee, and David Schumacher. *The Sheens: Martin, Charlie and Emilio Estevez*. London: Robson Books, 1991.

Sheen, Martin, and Emilio Estevez. *Along the Way: The Journey of a Father and Son*. New York: Free Press, 2012.

Straub, Gerry. *When Did I See You Hungry?* Cincinnati: St. Anthony Messenger Press, 2002.

Published interviews

Sheen, Martin. Interview by Dotson Radner. *Parade*. December 2, 2001.

Sheen, Martin. Interview by David Kupfer. *The Progressive*. June 30, 2003.

Sheen, Martin. Interview by James Lipton. *Inside the Actors Studio,* Bravo, August 10, 2003.

Sheen Martin. Interview by Rose Pacatte. "On the Way with Martin Sheen," *National Catholic Reporter*, October 7, 2011.

Unpublished interviews by Rose Pacatte

Bourgeois, Roy. July 29, 2014, Kihei, HI. Audio recording.

Buscema, Helena. July 24, 2014.

Chavez, Paul. August 13, 2014, Kihei, HI. Audio recording.

Clark, Matt. January 10, 2014. Culver City, CA. Telephone.

Dear, John. July 28, 2014, Kihei, HI.

Dietrich, Jeff, and Catherine Morris. August 13, 2014, Los Angeles, CA. Audio recording.

Estevez, Joe. July 18, 2014, Kihei, HI. Audio recording.

Estevez, John, and Frank Estevez. March 5, 2014, Dayton, OH. Audio recording.

Estevez Phelan, Carmen. February 2014–August 2014, Culver City, CA. Letters and email.

Kerze, William. April 22, 2014, Malibu, CA. Audio recording.

Kmiec, Douglas W. January 21, 2014, Culver City, CA. Email.

McAlister, Elizabeth. August 1, 2014, Kihei, HI. Email.

Rhodes, Michael. July 17–18, 2014. Email.

Rodriguez, Arturo S. August 12, 2014, Kihei, HI. Audio recording.

Schmidt, Ron. July 26, 2014. Audio recording.

Sheen, Martin. January 8, 2014, Malibu, CA, Audio recording.

Sheen, Martin. August 18, 2014, Culver City, CA.

Straub, Gerry. August 30, 2014, Culver City, CA.

Torgerson, Lloyd. July 18, 2014, Kihei, HI. Audio recording.

Ward, Carla. August 25, 2014, Culver City, CA.

Index